FAULTED

By

Jacqueline Druga

I0787831

Faulted - By Jacqueline Druga
Copyright 2018 by Jacqueline Druga

This is a work of fiction. Names, characters, places and incidents are either the product of the author's imagination or are used fictitiously, and any resemblance to any person or persons, living or dead, events or locales is entirely coincidental.

Paula Gibson and Kira R thank you both so much for all of your help and questions.

Also to my Beta Book Group … you all rock, Your feedback is invaluable.

Cover Art by Christian Bentulan
www.coversbychristian.com

ONE

'You suck,' the text message read. 'Bring home my son, CJ.'

First of all, CJ thought as he looked down to the phone. *He's my son, too.*

Bleep.

She was fast. CJ barely had time to start a reply before she sent another message. He wasn't good at texting, he always made mistakes. Often switching can't and can. Giving approval for things he didn't mean to.

He wondered if that was the main reason Kylie was flying off the cuff.

Maybe he wasn't clear. He should have listened to his father when he told him to turn it off.

CJ huffed. It was bad enough he was packed into the hotel lobby like a toy in one of those crane machines, but now he had to reply to her messages while keeping a diligent eye on his six-year-old son while his father was off wondering somewhere.

'I thought your flight left at two. Why are you not on the plane?'

"Are you kidding me?" CJ looked at his phone. "How many times have I already told you?" Are you that dense?"

"Excuse me?" a woman nearby responded.

"Oh, gees, sorry." he lifted his phone to show her. "Not you. My phone. Sorry." He stared at his keyboard and spoke under his breath, "It's two o'clock pacific time not eastern time." Then he simply replied. 'Two this time, not yours.'

There, he thought, that ought to do it. He looked down to his son, while the little guy shared CJ's name of Carter James, he didn't share the nickname. CJ refused to let that happen, and he insisted everyone call the child by his given name, Carter.

Although his father didn't listen.

Carter was in his own world sitting in the chair. They had just completed their male bonding, generation vacation to Disneyland finishing in Los Angeles. The first time Kylie let CJ take him on vacation let alone out of the state. It was just the three of them. The guys.

They were all wearing the same t-shirt. Carter sported a pair of big mouse, sparkling blue, 'Dazzle Me' headphones, his dad bought the same pair, he was even wearing them like Carter, but CJ made him take them off in public. Carter was occupied as he played with a small tablet. He was a good kid; quiet, often times a little backward. He was a little on the thick side, heavy for his age, with dark wavy hair that wasn't easy to manage.

Bleep.

"Oh, come on!" CJ blasted and lifted the phone.

"I told you to shut that thing off, didn't I? She hasn't stopped texting you," his father Guy, approached him from behind.

"It's not responsible for me to turn off the ..." CJ paused and sniffed. "Were you smoking weed?"

"I was. I had to get my blaze on before the plane."

"Oh my God."

"Had a little left and didn't want TSA sniffing me."

"They'll smell you now."

His father waved out his hand in a 'no worry' manner.

"Wait. Where did you get the weed?"

"The weed." He snickered. "It's easy. All depends who you know in the kitchen."

The phone beeped again.

"She's getting impatient," Guy pointed to the phone. "What does she want now? If she wants to know again if he pooped, tell her ..."

"Dad."

"Fine. She's just ridiculous."

CJ finally looked and read the message asking why they hadn't left the hotel. "Wanna know why, I'll show you why."

"Oh, I know why she's ridiculous, the sheer amount of absurd texts."

"No, she wants to know why we are still at the hotel. I'll show her." He lifted his phone and took a picture of the lobby,

A human barricade was set up with security men. Just as the Wynne men were about to leave four high security details showed up. It pissed off CJ because he had already checked out of the hotel with an hour left. He wanted to get a cab, get to the airport and get lunch.

Now all that was gone askew.

The cab driver showed up, he even called that he couldn't get into the driveway.

"No worries, dude, I can't get out of the hotel," replied CJ.

He was told it was only going to be a few minutes.

Last time he checked it had already been forty-five.

He sent the picture to Kylie with the words, "This is why. Personal security detail."

'Holy crap!' She replied with several exclamation points. 'Is it the president? The Queen?'

'No. Mindy Snow.'

'The aging pop star? Tell them she's not important enough to miss your flight for.'

At that point CJ was boiling. Couldn't she just pick up the phone? He could have told her he tried. CJ was better at talking on the phone, aside from making lots of text typos, he was pretty passive when text messaging.

'I'll try.' He wrote, then added, 'phone is gonna die'

It wasn't. He just was done.

And he was done waiting, too. It was pushing the time limits to make it through airport security and race across the terminal to the gate with a six year old and a near senior citizen to make the flight on time.

"Where are you going?" Guy asked.

"To get us out of here," he said.

CJ walked forward and approached the security guard. A younger guy, not too big. He looked more suited for the FBI with his tight black polo shirt and sunglasses.

"Hi, excuse me." He tapped him on the shoulder. "Oh, look you have a name tag, how cute. Roger. Excuse me, Roger. We really have to leave."

"It'll be a few more minutes."

"It was a few minutes, forty-five minutes ago."

"Miss Snow does not like anyone in the lobby when she comes through. She doesn't like the smell of alcohol or …" he sniffed. "Marijuana."

CJ lifted his shirt to smell it, he was going to kill his father.

"She'll be down shortly."

"Wait. Wait. She's been in this hotel? How is this the first time I saw you guys?"

"Maybe you weren't here, maybe …" He peered over to Carter lowering his sunglasses. "At Disneyland?"

"Maybe, but look, here's the deal," CJ said. "This is our first vacation together since me and his mom broke up. First. Actually, this is the first time I've been allowed to take him out of state. But … besides being stuck with my stoner father another day, if I don't get him home on time, if I miss the plane, if I blow this, well, my ex married a lawyer … so I'm screwed."

Roger exhaled heavily, looked at Carter then said, "Hold on." he walked over to talk to another guard.

CJ gave a thumbs up to Carter and his dad. Neither paid attention.

"Alright," Roger said as he returned. "Because I feel you as a single dad, and having a stoner father, I'll make you an offer. You can catch a ride to the airport with us, go through private security …. If … you tell everyone we went to high school together in Cleveland, don't throw me under the bus, and give me those sparkly blue, mouse headphones for my kid."

CJ looked at Carter. He wasn't about to rip the headphones from his son, but he certainly would from his father. "Deal." CJ held out his hand.

Roger shook his hand. "Don't go too far."

CJ lifted his hand signaling he promised he wouldn't and spun around. He hurried to Carter and tapped him on the leg. "Hey, check this out. We're getting a ride to the airport with the important people. Maybe I'll do a selfie with Mindy and your mom will get all jealous because I'm with a pop star."

Carter lifted his one ear from his headphone. "What's a pop star?"

"Don't worry about it." CJ placed Carter's headphones on again.

"How'd you manage that?" his father asked.

"Simple." CJ smiled. "Give me your Dazzle Me Headphones."

TWO

Ruben Beginski was used to being pre-judged. He had been a driver for a long time. His clients were upper class and generally they musically stereotyped him the second they stepped into his vehicle. They'd look at him and his olive complexion, hear the name 'Ruben', and jokingly say, "Can we not listen to that merengue music or salsa?"

They assumed because he looked Hispanic, that he was. Technically and genetically speaking, Ruben was Latino. However, by heritage, he was Polish and proud. He was adopted at age one by fantastic parents, and they gave him a smothering babci.

His entire childhood centered around keeping the Polish tradition. Even the food he ate. Ruben mastered cooking and made a mean Bigos.

He had never experienced any type of Mexican food until he was a freshman in high school when they served tacos.

Never did he find people's attitude toward him offensive. He was used to it and found it funny at times.

 He had a great sense of humor, he had to. He started driving his father's airport shuttle at the age of twenty-one, so he had seen all types of people come and go. Twenty-five years later, he was a private driver. He would have driven the airport shuttle until he himself retired, but his father ended up selling the business.

His current driving gig was an accident and a blessing … sort of. He didn't make a lot of money, but he saw the world.

He was picking up a client at Washington Dulles, a Senator. The Senator told Ruben he recommended him for a special, secret job, and asked if he were available. The driver who was supposed to do it was sick.

Ruben said, "Sure." Once he dropped the Senator off at the hotel, Ruben headed over to the Music Center and pulled around back.

He had no idea who he was picking up. At first he thought it was the scrawny guy who slipped into the back seat.

But it wasn't. That man was the instruction guy.

"Security will escort her into the car," he said. "They will shut the door. At no time are you to get out. Do not look at her or speak to her. Keep the privacy window up unless she puts it down. Take her straight to the hotel around back. Security will get her from the car. Again, no talking. Got that?"

"Sure."

"Good." He handed Ruben an envelope and left the car.

Once he was gone, Ruben started counting the money. He debated on taking a couple days off after seeing the amount of hundred-dollar bills. Fifteen to be exact. He was in the middle of enjoying it when he heard the crowd screaming. Before he could register what was going on, he set the envelope on the front passenger seat, the back door opened and they pretty much shoved her in.

He squinted in the rearview mirror to get a look.

He saw her for a few seconds. He recognized her right away. Mindy Snow. She was a hot mess. At one time she was an adorable teenager, singing songs for girls who wanted to be just like her when they grew up. As she grew up she tried to be more adult in her music, but no one took her seriously. Then she went on a complete spiral downhill. People still paid for her concerts, though. When he first met her, she was a thirty year old woman, a decade after her glory days, trying to be what she was in her youth. There she sat in his limo, her hair matted from sweat and hairspray, her eye makeup smeared under her eyes, wearing clothes too young for her and too tight for the weight she had gained in weird places.

Not long after the back car door closed and Ruben peeked at who it was, she slowly slid sideways and passed out on the bench seat.

Traffic around the music center was insane, and Ruben knew another way. It would take longer distance wise to get to the airport hotel, but shorter in time.

To Ruben, Mindy Snow wouldn't even notice, she was out of it. He tilted the mirror to watch her in case she rolled off the seat. It wasn't long into the drive before he noticed she hadn't moved. Even with the bumps in the road.

Against his instructions he lowered the privacy window. "Miss Snow?" he called to her. "Miss Snow?"

He did that a few times with no reaction from her and concerned he pulled over. He immediately went around to the back of the car and opened the door. A strong smell of urine and alcohol hit him as Mindy lay semi on her back. After calling out to her once more, he reached down to touch her. Her legs felt clammy and cooler, her skin color was pasty.

He closed the door, went around the passenger side nearer to her head. It was only a few seconds, but by the time he opened that door, not only was she vomiting, she had begun choking on her own regurgitation.

Ruben grabbed onto her immediately, first turning her to her side before raising her up and hitting her hard on the back several times.

The contents in her throat emerged and she coughed. Coughing was good, at least she was breathing.

Still, Mindy Snow was unconscious and any reaction was pure reflex. He thought about calling 911, but knew he was only a couple blocks from the hospital. He could get her there faster than calling for help.

He was fearful, after all it was Mindy Snow, and Ruben was sure her 'team' would not be happy. Instead of leaving her alone in the back with vomit and piss, he locked his arms under hers and pulled her from the back of the limo to the front passenger's seat. He sat her up and buckled her in.

The entire ride to the hospital was done, speeding, steering the wheel with one hand while holding her head up.

He peeled around to the emergency entrance, raced out of the car and to her door. He opened it, scooped her in his arms and ran inside.

"I need help. Someone please."

At first a security guard ran over, then a nurse.

"Get me a gurney," the nurse yelled out as she examined her. "Stat. My God, this is Mindy Snow."

"Yes, yes it is. She was in my limo."

"We got this. Do you have the number for her people?" the nurse asked when the cart arrived.

"No, I don't."

"We'll handle it. Put her down, thank you. On her side."

Barely had Ruben placed Mindy on the gurney and on her side, they were moving her. As they pushed through the door he watched, then he noticed his envelope of money was stuck like glue to Mindy's back side, adhered more than likely from the moisture.

He stayed for a little while, until they told him she was stable. She had alcohol poisoning and drugs in her system. They pumped her stomach and she was going to be alright. Perhaps it was bad timing, but he inquired about the money envelope.

"Look, I know this is going to sound shallow. But when I put her in the front seat, she sat on my pay envelope and it was stuck to her."

"You're right," the nurse said. "It is shallow. And I'll let her people know."

Mumbling, 'great' under his breath, he waited longer for her people. If they did show, they didn't come in the main door and Ruben left.

The next morning he received a call asking him to come to the hospital. The man identified himself as Jason, and he was the one who was in the limo before Mindy. Jason sounded angry and asked Ruben to come immediately to sign Non-Disclosure forms.

As much as he didn't want to go, Ruben did. Outside paparazzi swarmed and a security escorted him in right away. He was brought to the fourth floor and Jason, along with three others stood outside a door.

"First," Jason said. "Don't think for a second we're here to thank you for your heroism. Do you know what you did by bringing her here before calling us? It was an idiot move. You're an idiot."

Ruben refrained from saying anything, and even if he wanted to, he didn't get a chance.

"We have a Non-Disclosure for you to sign. You are not to speak to anyone about this." He shoved a clipboard in his chest. "Sign it."

"What?" Ruben asked.

"Sign."

"Look, my pay was stuck to her rear, can I get it back?"

"Fuck you! Fuck you!" Jason screamed. "You don't deserve shit right now. Look what you did to her! You're lucky we don't press charges against you. Feeding her alcohol and lord knows what other drugs."

"What?" Ruben asked again confused. "I did no …"

"You'll never work again as a driver," Jason blasted.

"Ever," the other man repeated.

"Never," said the third. "You'll lose all respect. You won't have a job."

At that second the door to the room flew opened and Mindy, wearing only a hospital gown, held her IV pole. "What the hell is going on out here?"

"Him!" Jason pointed. "We're just trying to get him to sign this form. No worries, Tab, he'll be gone and we will make sure he loses his job."

"Please do," she said. "Because I want him working for me."

"What?" Jason asked.

Ruben, wide eyed, looked at her.

"Do you know what he did?" she asked.

"Yes, he brought you here before waiting on us," Jason said.

"He saved my life. They told me I was minutes away from death. Minutes. I was choking on my own vomit, he saved me from that, and if ... if he waited for you, I would have died. So I want him working for me."

"He didn't follow the rules," Jason said. "He's a rule breaker."

"Thank God for that. He will work for me as my private driver in every city. I'm tired. I have a headache. I ... I'm stressed." She looked at Ruben and not only spoke loudly, she spoke slowly. "What ... is ... your ... llama?"

Ruben was confused by that.

"Ruben," Jason answered. "His name is Ruben."

Immediately, Mindy stepped to him and hugged him. "Ruben ... thank you for ... salvar ... my liftito." She stepped back, squeezed his arms and went back to her room.

"Wow," Ruben said.

Jason huffed loudly. 'Give me your contact information. I'll be in touch with all the employment contracts."

"Okay. But my pay from last night."

"Not my problem if you lost it, now is it?" Jason walked away.

He never did get that envelope of money, he needed to give it to his ex-wife for child support for their seventeen year old son. Luckily, she was pretty understanding considering not only was he all over the news, but he was going to be working for Mindy Snow.

That was six years earlier. And for six years he was her trusted driver in every city of every tour. They rented him a car to drive.

In all those years, Mindy never really got to know him. In fact, because he was a man of few words, she assumed he didn't speak English very well. Since the day she hired him, she always spoke loudly to him as if he were hard of hearing. Not only that, she claimed he helped her perfect her Spanish, she also took credit for teaching him English.

Where some would get offended, Ruben knew she didn't do it to be mean. She wasn't a racist or bigot, she just wasn't smart enough to realize it, her brain was fried. Ruben didn't help matters, after the first couple months, he stopped trying to tell her. Then he just found it amusing and figured she'd eventually realize the truth.

Six years later … she still hadn't.

She did however go from living on the edge to straight edge. She insisted those around her didn't consume alcohol or drugs in her presence with such insistence that it drove everyone nuts.

It didn't bother Ruben when she ranted or screamed at him about her team, he just pretended he didn't understand a word she said.

THREE

It was nowhere near as glamorous as CJ envisioned in his mind. When the security guy Roger said he'd be going with them to the airport, CJ thought wild times, a chance to see Mindy Snow up close and get a once in a lifetime photo op for his son. However, that was far from what happened. He was on shuttle three to the airport. Mindy was nowhere to be found, she was tucked safe and sound in a limousine Humvee that wasn't anywhere near them.

CJ didn't even get to ride with the band. He, his son, and father were in the shuttle that not only carried the second string dancers, it had crew like the cord wrapping guy and the woman that raced behind the scenes to wipe Mindy's sweat.

He was in the nobody of nobody bus.

Not that those people were really nobodies, they just weren't Mindy Snow.

His father, however, seemed to enjoy being in the company of the motley crew. The upbeat, talkative crew passed around a bottle of vodka, and huddled in the bathroom of the bus making a vain attempt to hide the fact that they were smoking weed through a vape.

"Guys," CJ told them, "We're in California. It's legal."

His father befriended them all, and was the person who made jokes that everyone found extremely funny. Except CJ.

In fact their antics bothered him when traffic went from a slow crawl to a dead stop. He was certain, private security or not, they weren't making their flight.

Maybe it wasn't his dad and the Mindy crew as much as the fact that he had to send a message to Kylie telling her they probably weren't making it home on the two PM plane.

CJ dreaded every single time he looked at his phone, because he didn't want to see how fast time was ticking by, nor did he want to see a return text from Kylie.

Carter groaned. "My battery's at twenty."

"Maybe you should stop playing with it. Save it."

"I'm bored."

"Me, too."

"What's going on?" his father made his way back to the row across from CJ. "When did we stop?"

"Fifteen minutes ago."

"Dad, I'm hungry," Carter said.

"I know, bud." He rubbed his head. "We should have eaten by now."

"You have snacks in your bag," Guy said.

"They're for the plane, Dad," CJ said.

"We can get more at the airport."

"If we ever get there." CJ clumped in his seat and looked at his phone. It was odd, he opened up his messaging.

Nothing.

"What's wrong?" Guy asked.

"I sent Kylie a text about how we're probably missing the flight. She didn't reply."

"You mean the same woman who sent you a text every fifteen minutes, every day."

"Strange." CJ sent her another message asking if she had received the previous one. He kept staring, waiting on a reply.

"Why don't you call her?"

"Yeah, that's a good idea. As much as I hate it, I have to let her know." CJ dialed and placed the phone to his ear. A few seconds later, he pulled it away. "It went straight to voice mail."

"Probably dead from all the texting."

CJ started dialing again.

"Who are you calling now?" Guy asked.

"Hating to do it, I'm calling the husband." CJ lifted the phone, then instantly pulled it back. "Odd. It went to voicemail as well."

"Doesn't he have a fancy office?" Guy asked. "Maybe try there."

"It's Saturday, I doubt they're in." CJ was about to call again when he leaned into the aisle. "I wonder if there's an accident or something." As soon as he got a clear look at the front of the shuttle, he turned to his father. "Where's the driver?"

Guy shrugged. "I don't know. I wasn't paying attention."

CJ stood. "I'm gonna see if I can find out what's happening. Keep an eye on him."

"I will."

"That means no partying in the bathroom." CJ pointed.

"I take offense to that. I raised you."

"Yes, that's why I'm telling you." CJ clipped into the short aisle, walking toward the front. No one on the crowded shuttle seemed to care or worry about the stand still traffic or the fact that the driver was gone.

Maybe the traffic was normal and CJ was just overreacting because it was so close to his flight.

Once outside the full extent hit him. He had been in traffic jams in the past, never ones where people stepped out of their cars.

Nothing was moving, cars had stopped their engines and the occupants of vehicles were out and about on the expressway. In impatient attempts to get by traffic, cars made an extra lane on the shoulder only to jam things up further.

There was something a little strange about it all.

People were checking their phones. Shaking their heads.

CJ didn't see the shuttle driver. He'd thought briefly that maybe he went somewhere to go to the bathroom, then realized that was unfeasible since they were on a raised section of the highway.

He looked left to right, but didn't see him. He did see the second shuttlebus a little farther up the road.

"Excuse me." He approached a man playing around with his phone. "Is there an accident? Do you know?"

"I don't. Sorry. Was trying to find out." He showed him his phone.

"Did you hear?" a voice in the distant said. "All flights east are cancelled."

"They can't cancel all flights, that's got to be wrong," someone else said.

CJ heard that and dismissed it, it didn't sound right. There was nothing on the news. No alerts on his phone. As he was about to go back to the shuttle, he saw the Humvee limo. The driver was standing by Roger the security guy outside the vehicle.

Changing direction, CJ approached the pair. "Hey Roger, you guys know what's going on?"

"No, I was just asking Ruben the same thing."

Ruben pulled a phone from his ear. "I was just trying to reach the first shuttle. They left about fifteen minutes before us. I thought they would have made it to the airport. No luck. They're stuck in traffic, too. I used to drive a lot in this city, I have never seen the 105 so bad. We've been sitting here so long, people are getting out of their cars."

"We lost our shuttle driver. And ... someone back there." CJ pointed. "They said all flights to the east are cancelled."

"That's insane," said Roger, "We'd have heard something. Something big is holding this up."

"It's freaky," said CJ. "I tried calling my ex out east and it went straight to voice mail. I hope something didn't happen out that way."

"It probably is an accident," Ruben said. "A big one. Maybe even a pile up. Might be worth taking a look on a local news site. Something like this is bound to make the news."

Suddenly, and with urgency, the rear door of the limo burst open and Mindy jumped out screaming horrifically. "Oh my God! Ruben!"

Ruben and Roger rushed toward her.

Did something happen? What was wrong?

Mindy appeared scared and confused as she held her phone, turning left to right.

"What is it?" Roger asked. "What's wrong?"

"Oh my God," she sobbed. "I can't post. It won't let me update." Her words shook as she spoke, rushed. "I made a ... typo!

My poor fans. I hit post after I wrote, 'help, I'm stuck', I can't change it." She growled out a sob as if someone died and with her crying, nearly dropped to her knees. "There's no connection!"

Ruben blinked hard and swung his head her way. "What?"

"Are you serious?" Roger asked. "This is the reason for all the dramatics."

"You don't understand!"

"No! I don't. You scared the hell out of me!"

"My phone."

"Holy shit." Roger blasted. "This is insane behavior. Ruben tell her."

CJ watched and tried his hardest not to laugh. Initially he worried that she learned devastating news, but once he realized it wasn't the case, he held back laughter.

"Ruben," she turned to him. "Can you fix … my … phone?"

Ruben took it.

Roger told her, "Get back in the car."

"It's hot in there," she said.

"Get back in the car … the paparazzi … they may see you." Roger raised an eyebrow.

"Shit." She spun around quickly and the moment she did …

Boom.

The loud sound caused an immediate and frightening silence. It clearly wasn't an explosion, it was more of a sonic boom. Like something had broken the sound barrier.

Just as the sound caught CJ's attention, a slight vibration occurred, causing a clattering noise as the air appeared to ripple.

Instantly he panicked, as he took one step to return to his son on the shuttle the ground began to shake.

It started mildly, then it quickly built with intensity.

The section of 105 where they had come to a standstill was on a raised section. It hovered over the street below by twenty feet, and as CJ raced for the shuttle, the highway swayed like a roped bridge.

He couldn't keep his balance, every few seconds he fell to the ground and fought to stand again.

The rumbling was loud, causing pressure in his ears. As he spotted the shuttle, he then saw his father holding Carter tight in his arms. They had gotten out.

Just as the thought, 'Thank God' came to his mind in relief, a loud crack jolted the road.

Guy turned his head to his left, then wide-eyed he leapt forward in the nick of time. The shuttle and the cars before and after it dropped out of sight as that part of the overpass collapsed.

Debris flew through the air, surrounding buildings dropped like matchsticks, and shattered glass flew through the air raining down all around.

CJ bolted their way, grabbing onto them as the three of them tried with diligence to stay standing.

Carter's screams were muffled in his grandfather's hold and the noise of the quake. CJ knew his son was scared, he had to be. He just held on to them. The only way off that overpass was to drop with the road, and if that was going to happen, it would happen to them all.

Ruben saw Roger try to grab for Mindy, but he wasn't fast enough or close enough.

Surely it had to be panic that caused her to jump back in the Humvee the second the earthquake started. She jumped in and shut the door.

What was she thinking?

Ruben flung open the back door, inside Mindy fought frantically to put on a seatbelt.

"You can't stay in here." Ruben shouted.

"Shut the door. Shut the door."

He extended his arm in to get her, but another jolt of the ground sent him flying inside and the Humvee door slammed as Ruben landed on Mindy.

He barely had time to understand or register everything she screamed at him when the hardest quake hit. It was a shock of the ground like no other.

Ruben knew exactly what it meant. He felt the Humvee bounce upward and move.

The road below them had given out. He was expecting it.

He clutched the armrest on the door handle and grabbed onto her as the vehicle flipped upward and went airborne... But his grip wasn't strong enough when the Humvee came down and impacted front end first.

Mindy flew forward, careening into the privacy window, it held her without breaking, Ruben gripped to the seat for dear life as he dangled above her. The ground finally stopped shaking and the Humvee came to a halt resting upright on the front bumper.

Ruben wasn't sure where they landed or if they were trapped, but he knew one thing … they were alive.

FOUR

Boom.

"No," CJ thought. "Not again. Please not again."

It was the same sound.

Carter cried. Cradled now in his arms, the boy locked his legs around CJ's waist, he held tightly to his neck and wept. He was scared, and rightfully so. CJ wondered how one even begun to comfort a child, when his mind was just focused on protecting him.

With each passing second that became an increasingly difficult feat.

Moments before, CJ, his father, Carter and Roger, did the only thing they could do. They ran. Rushing forward as the section of highway they had been on crumbled to the ground below taking with it every vehicle and person on the road.

They were on steady solid ground, the emotional cries of post trauma screams, along with car alarms filled the air. CJ was grateful to still be standing when the second sonic boom occurred.

This time, for some reason, holding tight to Carter, he spun to the sound and looked up.

He saw it. A flash in the sky, and ever so quickly, he swore he saw a light sail overhead.

He braced himself and his son.

There was really nowhere to run. Behind them was a drop off, ahead of them, more highway that could collapse.

He waited, trying to think of how to hold on to steady ground while holding on to his child.

There was a vibration, the ground rumbled a bit, nothing like the previous quake … then nothing.

CJ released the breath he held.

"My God," his father gasped out the words.

CJ turned. He saw his father stranding near the edge of the broken highway, looking down.

"Dad," CJ said. "Step back. Please."

"Oh my God, CJ. Look at this."

Hand cupped to the back of Carter's head, CJ inched his way there. He was scared to get too close. Scared that another jolt of the ground could send him and his child toppling down.

He could only imagine what his father looked at. Around them, structures and buildings had toppled, debris was tossed about the highway. When he finally looked below, he saw a cavern filled with cars. Body parts emerged between the wreckage.

CJ felt instantly sick to his stomach.

"They're down there," Roger's voice was close.

CJ didn't know who 'they' was at first until he saw the Humvee limo below, balancing on its front end. It wasn't stable, at least it didn't look it. It could fall at any time. It was on top of a car that had been smashed like a tin can.

"Help me," Roger said with desperation. "Will you help me?"

At first CJ didn't know who Roger spoke to, then he realized it was him. "Help you?"

"Yes, please. We have to help them. There are people down there." Roger moved to the edge. "Please."

It wasn't that far down to get to the heap of automobiles. A four foot fall, maybe slightly more. But at what cost? What was going to happen the second the weight of their bodies landed on the cars below? If there were people alive down there, would they make it worse?

Although Roger intended on helping anyone he could, CJ was certain his primary focus was on the Humvee limo.

Roger got down to the ground, turned and feet first started to climb down.

"I'll help you," Guy said and stepped forward.

"No." CJ stopped him. "I'll go. Stay with Carter."

"You stay with your son."

"Dad, no," CJ insisted. He couldn't with a clear conscious let his father go down there. Even though his father was a strong man,

CJ was younger. He stood less chance of getting hurt. He peeled Carter from his embrace. "Go with Pap." He handed the child over.

Carter immediately gripped Guy.

"Be careful," Guy told him.

CJ nodded and followed Roger, doing the same as he did, lowering himself feet first to the area below.

The steel girders of the broken highway extended out, adding to the danger.

The moment CJ's feet rested on the wreckage of a car, he heard a 'thump' beneath him. He looked down. Just by his feet was a side window of an automobile. Two hands hit against the glass.

"Help me," a woman called out, muffled. "Help." She banged against the glass some more.

Why didn't the window break? He couldn't even see the rest of the car, only that window. The door wasn't accessible.

"Dad!" CJ yelled up. "Dad, find me something to break glass."

"I'll look!" Guy replied.

"Stay here with her," Roger said, "I'm going to check the Humvee."

CJ nodded. He couldn't clearly see the woman's face, but he signaled her with his hand, palms up, conveying for her to hold on, he would do the best he could.

The interior of the limo wasn't like a lot of other Humvee limos. It didn't just have two long bench seats, it also had two swiveling bucket seats. Ruben was able to grasp one for support as he figured out how to help Mindy right below him. He had to be careful. He was confident in the strength of the privacy glass, but still didn't want to take a chance adding his weight to it. It seemed everything that wasn't secure in the back of the limo had crashed forward onto Mindy. Slowly he allowed himself to drop forward, landing his feet on the section below the window.

"Mindy," he called to her. "Mindy."

She didn't respond.

He nudged his foot to her and she groaned.

Ruben knew the limo was balancing. He didn't know if it was steady or could topple over any minute.

"Mindy," he called her again.

She partly rolled over, knocking bottles and glasses from her. Her forehead had a huge gash that bled badly.

"Hey," he said to her, slowly crouching down.

She opened her eyes.

Ruben smiled at her. "Don't move. I'll get you out."

He looked behind him and reached for the handle of the front rear driver's door. The handle unlatched, but the door wouldn't budge. Holding on to the rear seat, he slowly crept across to the passenger side door. Grabbing onto the handle, he pulled it, then pushed on the door. It moved four inches out and stopped.

Ruben grunted in frustration and closed his eyes to think.

"Ruben," the voice called.

His eyes popped open and widened. "Roger?"

"Yeah, man, you okay?"

"I'm fine. I'm fine."

"Mindy?"

"She has a head injury," Ruben said. "I think she'll be okay. Hard to tell." He looked at her. "The door's jammed."

"Yeah, you're sandwiched in here."

"Are we gonna topple over?" Ruben asked.

"I think you're wedged pretty good."

"Any ideas?"

"I'm going to find something to break a window," Roger said. "We'll get you out that way."

"Thank you."

"Just hang tight. Leave this open for some air."

"I will." Ruben paused. "Roger, how bad is it?"

"It's bad, man. It's bad. Hang tight."

Even though Roger couldn't see him, Ruben nodded.

Again, he crouched down and moved over to check on Mindy.

"You'll be okay," he said to her.

Another groan, then Mindy coughed. "Ruben."

"Yes."

She lifted her hand slowly toward him, in it, she still gripped her phone. "I can't see …" she said. "Do I have a signal yet?"

Ruben didn't answer. He gently pushed her hand back down and inched his way back to the door opening to wait on Roger.

FIVE

People were abandoning their cars in exchange for getting to safe ground. Walking away in the direction of the airport, which was only about two thousand feet west. Not a far walk at all. But was there really any safe place to go? The street level was a hazard zone, it had happened so fast there were no sirens in the background. Just panicked cries for help and people calling out names, looking for loved ones. Guy supposed the airport could be a safe place, a gathering place, a shelter for those who weren't from the area, and would suggest that to CJ after his son helped those in the trapped cars.

While Guy did see the arm or leg protruding from the wreckage that had dropped from the overpass, he imagined many people were stuck in their cars, injured and unable to get out. They were pieced together tightly.

Carter was a heavy boy and it was hard carrying him around, Guy did his best, he only set him down when he checked out the cars.

"Stay close. Hold on to my belt loop," Guy told him.

Carter did. The headphones were still draped on his neck, his backpack on his back.

The best tool needed to break a window and accessible was a tire iron. Now Roger had yelled up that he needed one, too.

Guy popped the trunk of a Subaru with the keys that were left in the ignition. He was able to find the spare tire kit and grabbed the iron from there.

He walked over to the edge and tossed it to CJ, yelling to Roger, "I'll grab another." He turned around again, walking back to the abandoned cars, looking for a newer model, knowing that tools were standard in the trucks. It wasn't hard to find another tire iron, this one a little sturdier.

He brought it to the edge and dropped it down to Roger who

was by the Humvee Limo. Guy wasn't sure if the tire iron would break the windows of the Humvee.

After that, he lifted Carter who had been anxious. His back pained some from the boy's weight.

"Would you be okay if I set you down and held your hand real tight?" Guy asked him.

"I guess."

"You guess no or yes?"

"Okay."

He slid the boy down to the ground and just as he took Carter's hand, he heard a massive amount of screaming coming from behind him. He turned to face the highway.

The screams grew louder and closer. Guy saw them. People. They ran fast and furious his way. Then he saw why. Behind them, in pursuit, was a wall of water.

◇◇◇◇

How tough is this glass? CJ wondered as he struck the window a second time.

"Stay back!" he yelled to the woman.

On the third attempt the window finally shattered.

He smiled in his victory, then the smile dropped at the same time he released the tire iron.

Loud, horrifying screams carried to him. When he looked up he had to duck. People were running full speed, and with nowhere to go, they dropped off the ledge. Bodies rained down around him, and CJ scooted back out of the way. They landed with thumps and cracks as their bones snapped upon impact.

"What the hell?" CJ spoke aloud.

There were two drink tables center of the limo interior. Both of them bolted strong to the floor. Like a scene from the Poseidon Adventure, Ruben had to nearly lift Mindy to the first table. So she could sit on the edge and be away from the broken glass and bottles.

A woman who had long since given up alcohol smelled like a local bar, every type of liquor had spilled on her.

"You got it?" he asked.

"Yes." She struggled, pulling herself up.

"Maybe if you put down the phone." He felt the weight lift.

"Made it."

No sooner was she up there, Ruben heard the sound of muffled screams coming from outside.

"What is that?" she asked. "What is happening? Is there a monster?"

Ruben would have labeled that comment ridiculous, until the limo jolted with loud thumps and bangs against it.

He believed debris was falling on them, little did he know it was actually people.

He hurriedly scooted to the slightly open door.

"Roger!" he screamed out. "Roger. What's going on?"

Roger placed his face close to the crack. "Oh my God, Ruben. Oh my God."

There was nowhere to run. He couldn't go back, he couldn't go forward. Guy clutched as tight as he could to Carter, taking refuge by a car to avoid the mob that rushed by them. Had he not moved he would have been caught in a stampede.

The time was near and he knew it.

A cool mist was in a wind that whipped his way, and the roar of water buried the screams. It didn't look that big in the distance. Maybe ten feet. But Guy knew two feet of rushing water could topple a man.

There was no escape.

He held on to Carter as he spun through a wheel of emotions. From scared to resolved.

"I love you so much, Little Man, I love you."

Carter moaned out a frightened, "Pap."

"Don't look. Don't look" Guy buried Carter's face to his chest. He looked once more than closed his eyes just before the wave arrived and blasted into them.

The question of what was causing the commotion, came to CJ before he could register.

First the people fell and then the water rushed forth.

It carried him only a few feet where he slammed into the underbelly of an upright truck that was wedged in the wreckage. Trying to catch his breath, his body caught up in the current, CJ lucked out.

Using the force of the water, he pivoted in toward the bed of the truck. As long as the truck didn't get swept away, the bed acted as some sort of shield.

The limo jolted hard, causing Mindy to tumble from her safe seat on the table. Just before she fell off completely, she caught herself.

"What's going on?"

Ruben grabbed for her legs to give her a boost when he saw the water rushing in.

"Oh my God!" Mindy screamed.

"Get up there." While pushing her, Ruben saw. The hand … it had to belong to Roger. He was desperately gripped to the edge of the door.

He wouldn't hold on for long and Ruben knew it.

"Try to make the next table," Ruben yelled as he dove for the door.

He reached through grabbing Roger's wrist and Roger grabbed his hand.

The pressure of the water pushed his arm against the door and Ruben knew it wouldn't take much more and his arm would break.

The water began at his ankles, filling up quickly, making it to his waist.

Mindy screamed, and Ruben took a deep breath just as the water crept from his chest to his chin, eventually burying him. But he still held on to Roger.

No amount of human strength could compare to the force of a raging wave of water, but Guy tried. He knew the second he was hit by the blast of water, it was game over.

He thought of the best way to angle his body when it hit him. If the water hit him in the back, surely it would cause his arms to release. He couldn't chance the force of it hitting Carter, so he turned slightly when it arrived and it slammed into his side.

As he feared, no matter how hard he tried to clutch his grandson, the water was more powerful. His arms released as the water took hold and he felt Carter slip from his embrace.

He was fast, faster than he believed he could be.

He reached out, grabbing Carter by the shirt and purchased a grip, on the fabric.

The water carried them fast and furiously. He pulled the shirt, bringing himself closer to Carter and was able to swing his other hand around, grabbing the boy's wrist.

He had him.

His fingers cramped as he held on tightly.

It seemed like forever. The water bringing both of them down, then back up. It probably was less than a minute, but underwater, with no warning to hold his breath, it felt like an eternity.

They moved with the current that was filled with debris. Even if he was able to call to Carter, there was no way the child would hear him.

Guy couldn't see enough to keep checking on Carter to see if he was alright.

All he could do was pray.

"God please, give me strength. Don't let me let go. Please let me hold on," he begged. "Please."

SIX

With a loud heaving breath, Ruben's head emerged from the water. He cleared the wetness from his eyes. Mindy was safely above the water line. Ruben estimated about six feet of water made its way in. But in order to hold onto Roger, he had to be submerged.

His arm thumped and a constant pain radiated through him. He was certain he had fractured it. Even broken, he held on to Roger as much as he could, but then he lost Roger's hand.

He was certain though, Roger made it. At the point he had to release, the water stopped rushing madly.

It was still in the Humvee, whether or not it moved outside.

"Give me your hand," Mindy reached down to him.

Ruben shook his head. "I'm good." He was at the point now that he could stand, the water came to his waist. He looked up toward the rear end. Why was it so dark in the vehicle? Surely one of the windows would have let some sunlight in tinted or not. He was trying to figure out how he was going to get up to the second set of rear doors. The bench seating made it impossible to get a footing.

There was no way he was going to be able to climb up to the hatch, especially with his arm.

"Are you alright?" Mindy asked.

"Yes." Reuben nodded. "My arm. It's broke."

"We have to get you to a hospital."

"You, too."

She looked at him curiously.

Ruben pointed to his own head.

She lifted her fingers to her forehead. "Ow."

"Yeah."

"Feels like a gash."

"Looks it, too," Ruben said, then exhaled. "We have to get out of here." To him, it was easier said than done. Plus, he didn't know what was outside the vehicle. The partially cracked door was completely submerged, so it was useless to yell out of that.

"Hey, Ruben?" Mindy called. She sat on the edge of the table staring forward. "Is there anything here we can use to open this sun roof? I can see straight out. Maybe if we open it I can climb out and get help."

Ruben's eyes widened. The sunroof. He didn't even think of it. He didn't need to find anything, it was a possible way out.

"Was that too many words?" she asked. "Did you understand what I said?"

"Yes," he said frustrated then smiled, speaking through his pain. "Mindy. There's … there's an emergency latch."

"This red thing here?" She asked.

Ruben nodded.

Mindy pulled the lever and the window popped.

"Push it out," Ruben told her.

Mindy shoved on the square window and it lifted and popped out. "I did it!" she excitedly yelled. "I'll go get help." She grabbed on to the window and hoisted herself up, then stopped. "Uh oh."

"Uh oh … what?"

She peered down to him. "I don't think there's going to be any hospital to go to."

Ruben was fearful of what she meant, but she braved the window and climbed out.

CJ had found protection, nestled securely in the bed of the truck, the water rushed by him and he felt safe. Until he realized the water brought debris with it.

The truck was a like a large rock in a stream, the water moved around it, then something slammed into the truck and it collapsed, sending CJ back into the wreckage beneath him, hitting his head.

He could feel the blood pouring out, there was nothing he could do.

There was space between him, the truck and the rushing water, but if he moved, it would be deadly. He knew he was fortunate enough to have air and he wasn't completely submerged. Trying to keep his wits about him, CJ realized his best bet was to stay put.

Stay until the loud sound of water had subsided.

And that was what he did.

It felt like forever, but CJ was certain it was not.

When he felt the pressure subside and the sound of the water quiet, he slipped between the edge of the truck and debris, squeezing through.

Once out he rolled to his hands and knees, his head pounded and as he looked down, he saw drops of blood fall into the water.

It was his blood.

He stumbled to a stand, and everything spun around him. Trying to catch his balance, he grabbed onto the truck to steady himself, that was when he got a good look.

More cars had piled up on top of the already smashed cars, the water moved steadily but slow, and had to be at least three or four feet deep.

When he had his wits about him, it hit him.

The woman in the car.

He made his way over, remembering well where he was when the water hit. He was just below the broken roadway.

He found the car, nothing had fallen on top of it, but that didn't matter.

CJ had broken the window to free the woman, but before he could do that, the water came. That broken window was an opening for the water to enter.

She didn't make it.

CJ could see her in the car. It was full of water.

The woman had drown. He turned away, when he did he saw Mindy hang drop from the Humvee SUV.

"CJ!" he heard his name called.

He looked around.

Roger was waving. "I need help with Ruben. He's still stuck."

CJ nodded. "Let me get my …" He paused. He hadn't even considered the fact that something had happened to his father and son. Why would it? They were safe on the road above. Surely the water was beneath them.

Before he finished his sentence, CJ spiraled into a state of panic. Suddenly that ledge above him seemed so far away and unattainable. He raced about the wreckage, his feet splashing in the water until he could find a way to climb up.

He found a way, using the cars that had tumbled. CJ made his way back up to the roadway.

The entire climb he begged in his mind that they'd be standing there.

When he reached the road … he saw nothing.

Not a person stood there.

It was empty.

Wet and empty.

Feeling as if his chest collapsed, CJ grabbed onto his knees and tried to catch his breath and slow his heart.

"Please, no. Please no," he said, then inhaled deeply and hollered as loud as he could. "Carter! Dad!"

Frantically he raced about looking over the road to the water below. He yelled and yelled, calling their names in complete desperation.

There was no reply.

His father and Carter were gone.

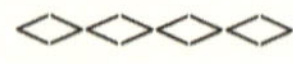

They had been pulled by the current for some time.

Guy was unable to stop or control where they went.

All he knew was he still had his grandson in his grip as the waters carried them away.

It wasn't an easy route, nor a painless one.

Floating with the water, Guy's legs smashed against rocks and other items buried in the water. Each hit sending a barrage of pain into his legs, arms, chest, wherever it hit.

More than once he went under.

But never did he loose contact with Carter.

To him, it was nothing short of a miracle that he was able to hold on. He didn't know where the wave would take them, but the rush and intensity of it subsided enough for him to catch his footing and sloppily stand.

The current was still strong, pushing against the backs of his legs.

He had no idea where they were, but he had stopped, and when he did, he pulled Carter to him.

As soon as he brought Carter into his chest, the boy's head dropped back.

"No. No." Guy brought his hand to Carter's face, shaking him. "Carter, baby. Carter."

The child's arms dropped lifelessly, he wasn't breathing.

Guy looked around. He had to get out of the water, he had to get the boy to a dry area. He spotted an area off to his left. The rubble of a building created a mound of bricks and Guy made his way there.

He trudged against the current, and with each step he examined Carter. Had he been injured? Hit by something?

Every ounce of physical pain Guy had felt was now gone, It was camouflaged by this fear for his grandson's life.

They had made it through the earthquake, the impact of the wave. They both were carried away. How was it even fair that the child was still attacked to his backpack, yet lost his life?

It wasn't happening. It couldn't be happening.

Finally, Guy made it to the area free from water, climbed the rubble and lay Carter down.

There was no heartbeat, no breaths.

Instantly, Guy's heart broke and he cried out loudly from his gut and grabbed onto the boy.

He repeated the word, "no", over and over as he clutched Carter to his chest.

He was panicked, scared, but he decided he wasn't giving up.

Despite the odds, Guy was able to hold onto Carter through the raging water, yet somehow, along the way he lost him.

But Guy wasn't giving up, not that easily. There was a reason he was able to hold Carter through it all, and it wasn't just for him to die.

Holding onto that thought, Guy place Carter on the bricks. It wasn't over. Not yet. Then Guy proceeded to do all that he could, give all that he had to try to bring Carter back.

SEVEN

It was controlled hysterics, Ruben could tell it was taking everything for CJ to keep it together. It was completely understandable. His father and son had been washed away.

As a father, Ruben knew the anguish of how CJ felt. The only reason Ruben wasn't concerned about his son was because he lived in Texas.

CJ searched frantically in the fallen wreckage, and Ruben hoped he didn't find them. Not there. Not in that mess.

It was internal chaos for all of them. Except maybe Mindy. She actually showed a human side, but didn't know what to do or how to help.

"Carter! Dad!" CJ yelled.

"They're not here," Roger told him.

CJ ignored him.

"Dude, they are not here."

"How do you know? I have to keep looking."

"The water man," Roger said. "It was powerful. I'm sorry. I'm not saying they aren't alright, I'm just saying it took them."

"One point eight miles," Mindy said. "Approximately. Which is nine thousand, six hundred and sixty-two feet, or three thousand, six hundred and eighty-four steps. Approximately."

The three men turned and looked at her.

Mindy closed her eyes, touched her fingers against her thumb as if counting. "Yes, that's correct. So it shouldn't take long at all to walk ..."

"Stop." Roger held up his hand. "Where are you getting that from?"

"Tsunami's move on land about twenty miles an hour. I counted three hundred and thirty-three seconds that water rushed into the limo. So that's how long the wave rushed through. With the current, they were brought that far until they slowed down. They aren't here they are …"

"One point eight three miles," CJ said.

"West." Mindy nodded.

"How did you figure that out so fast?" CJ asked.

"I have this knack for math," she replied. "I was told it was because I was probably artistic."

"Autistic," Roger corrected.

"That's what I said." She turned to CJ. "I'll help you look. I'll walk with you." She then faced Ruben. "But you have to find help for that arm."

"Your head, too," Ruben said.

"I'll be fine. He's bleeding, too." She pointed to CJ, "So together we're okay."

"I … I …" Roger stammered. "Don't even know how to react to that statement. I don't think right now there's help to be found. Not yet. We have people out here on this highway. A slew of them. I need to look for them."

"I'll help," Ruben said.

"We'll find something to brace your arm," Roger told him. "Until we can figure out where help is."

"How will we know?" CJ asked.

"Siren," Mindy replied. "Once you hear the sirens, emergency workers are out. There's an emergency plan for earthquakes."

"It wasn't an earthquake," CJ said. "I saw something streak across the sky."

Roger shook his head. "It couldn't be a meteor, something that shook the ground that hard would have been close, and there's no fireball. There'd be a fireball on impact."

"Well, I saw something."

"I'm not saying you didn't. And we're wasting time," Roger said. "Me and Ruben will look for our people and do what we can here. We should plan to meet back up. I mean, what happens if your father and son come here looking for you while you're out there?"

"You have a point," CJ said.

"We'll leave a note," Ruben said. "If we leave. In the limo."

"We'll find a way," Roger added. "If we aren't here, we'll find a way to let you know. Just look in the limo. I'm sure one of these cars has something to write on. A mile doesn't take that long to walk. We'll be back in three hours so check in. Okay?"

CJ agreed, then faced Mindy. "You don't have to come with me. It's alright."

"You shouldn't walk alone. Ruben is injured. I don't mind. I want to help find your son."

"Thank you." CJ began to walk.

"Three hours," Roger reiterated.

Ruben stood, water to his calves, watching CJ walk slightly ahead of Mindy. She carried her purse crisscross over her chest, it never left her body the entire ordeal. Nor did that phone leave her hand. And as she walked, she held that phone up looking at it, still trying to get a signal.

"Breathe!"

Guy wasn't particularly a religious man, but he was in that moment. Rubble surrounding him, everything blocked out in his focus, his only grandson laying lifeless on a mound of concrete, Guy prayed more in those moments than he had in his entire life.

"God please, don't take him from me. Please bring him back … breathe." He did everything he had learned about trying to save a drowning victim. It seemed as if he was doing compressions and giving breaths forever. The amount of time was lost in his heartache.

"Breathe."

Guy continued.

He went from praying to begging. Bartering his very own soul in exchange for the six year old boy.

"Take me. Just take me. Bring him back. Please … breathe."

Somewhere in it all, at some point, Carter coughed. When he did, water ejected from his mouth and as Guy lifted him upward he began to vomit.

Guy emotionally cried out and then gleefully embraced the boy, so happy, so grateful.

He whispered a 'Thank you' as he lifted his eyes to the sky and held Carter.

Carter began to cry.

"I know. I know." Guy held him. "I'm here. I have you."

Then it hit Guy. What now? Movies showed the revival of a victim, but what happened afterward? Did they just stay alive? Did they need further help before they reverted back? Guy didn't know if Carter would relapse.

He had been dead.

That was for sure. Now he was back.

The only thing Guy knew for certain was he needed to get help. He had to get medical attention for Carter.

The child was pale and clammy. He kept coughing and coughing. Guy supposed he would for a while until he ejected all water from his lungs.

The water was dirty as well. Surely if he didn't get Carter to a hospital he would get pneumonia.

Guy looked around. He was in a foreign city, unknown territory. He didn't have a clue where he was and even if he did, there were no distinguishable landmarks. Everything was flattened or nearly flattened.

The water was calmer, but it was still there, it hadn't receded yet.

Along with Carter, Guy worried about his own son. Was CJ okay? Was he alive? Did he survive that blast of water? The last time he saw his son he was below the highway.

More than anything Guy wanted to lift Carter and head back. Follow the water in reverse to the freeway and the section he last saw his son.

The father in him wanted and needed to do that. The father in him also knew, CJ would want his son taken care of.

Following the water back from where it came meant heading into a flooded area. If there was help out there, it wasn't there.

Dry land, out of the destruction was Guy's best bet.

He would walk along the water, following the flow until he stopped. Eventually he'd find out.

There was no one around, at least no one he could see, but that didn't mean there weren't survivors. Guy knew there had to be.

He would search out help after he gained some of his strength back. He was weak from the emotional trauma, and physically in pain from the bangs and bumps he took on the wave. He felt short of breath and his hands shook.

A few minutes, that was all he needed, then he would lift Carter and carry him.

Until then, he would just hold the child, take a moment and bask in the fact that he was alive.

EIGHT

When he was sixteen years old, Ruben broke his big toe. It was the worst pain he had felt in his life until that moment. His broken arm throbbed. Using a piece of wet wood from debris and his button down limo shirt, Roger helped him make a splint. It didn't help much, so Ruben self medicated with an unbroken bottle of scotch that was in the Humvee.

It wasn't like when he broke his toe, or even sliced his hand. There was no hospital to run to. No doctor in sight. As the minutes ticked by Ruben was just one of many who were injured. In fact, his injury was minor compared to a lot of others.

The more he and Roger searched for members of the Mindy Snow team, the more people they ended up helping.

Aiding them out of a trapped car, from under rubble and bringing them to a dry area off the road. Those who were strong enough to help did. And those uninjured who couldn't move wreckage searched the wreckage for anything they could use for first aid.

Eventually, help would come. Emergency workers, FEMA or even the military. When news broke of the disaster, aid would come.

It wasn't that long since CJ and Mindy walked off in their search, yet, Ruben was surprised with technology and the way news travelled, there wasn't a single news chopper flying overhead.

There was simply a feeling of abandonment.

Were they on their own?

What if help didn't come?

He thought about what CJ had said, that he saw a meteor. Roger said it was after the first quake and dismissed it as impossible because there hadn't been a fireball. What if CJ was correct and the meteor he saw wasn't the only one. A first strike elsewhere causing the quake and the second caused the wave.

As he one handedly dug through the debris, Ruben's mind raced with all sorts of scenarios. With everything around him destroyed, it felt like the end of the world. He reasoned that many who had been through similar disasters probably felt the same way. That life as they knew was over and some sort of apocalypse was upon them.

Ruben continued his searching and tried to dismiss those thoughts, but with each passing minute, and every dead body he uncovered, those thoughts were more predominant.

Walking the two miles, following the water, sounded easier than it was. It wasn't straight, flat land. What was buried under the water was unstable, and CJ lost his balance several times. He supposed the head injury didn't help. His head pounded ten times worse than any hangover he had ever experienced, he was dizzy and his stomach was queasy, flopping every few steps. After fifteen minutes, continuing on in the water wasn't an option. He had been in it long enough he could feel his skin shrivel and his feet began to burn in his shoes from being wet.

They moved to the side of the water, walking along the area that had been completely flattened.

Mindy walked ahead of him, she kept staring at her phone and every few feet would announce, "Nothing yet."

Not long into the walk, the ground shook.

It sent CJ into an instant panic. So much so, he felt the urge to run. When he did, his leg twisted, he sailed to the ground, and before he could get back up, he vomited uncontrollably.

"Aftershock," Mindy said, then noticed him on the ground and rushed over.

"I'm fine."

"No, you're not. Let's sit down."

"We haven't walked that long."

"Take a minute." She extended her hand to him.

He took it and used her as leverage to stand and she walked with him to find a place to sit. He hadn't a clue what he was sitting on, it was hard and it felt good to stop.

"Stay put," she told him.

"Where are you going?"

"We need to find water. I know that sounds weird. But you can't drink that." She pointed to the water.

"I … I kinda figured that."

"I'll be right back."

"Do you know where we are?" CJ asked.

"LA."

"No, I mean where?"

"I have an idea. But … it's really hard to say right now … where."

Mindy walked off and another tremor hit, she swayed in her walk. CJ gripped the debris that he sat on. The shaking ground was unnerving and something he didn't think he'd get used to.

He watched her for a while, she peeked in car wreckage, around and under, then he couldn't focus on her anymore, the farther she went, the blurrier she became.

She wasn't gone long, and when she returned she carried a dirty black, back pack looped over her shoulder and two bottles of water clasped in the fold of her arm.

"Take one," she told CJ when she returned.

He grabbed a bottle. "Where did you get these?"

"A car. This is LA, someone had bottled water."

He looked at it. "Expensive stuff, too."

"I checked out the expensive cars. One of them …. was a rental."

"How do you know?" he asked.

"I found this?" She reached behind her.

"What's in the bag?"

"Not much. More water, but I figured we could use it, pick up things along the way."

"That's good thinking."

"I'm quick like that. So …" she sat down. "This is what I found and how I knew it was a rental." She unfolded a map.

"This is of Los Angeles."

"Yes, it is. Anyone who lives here uses GPS. Which by the way is down."

"That's good to know," CJ said.

"Yeah. So … this is good to have."

"Any idea where we are on this?"

"Somewhere in this vicinity." She ran her finger in a circle on the map. "Not far from the airport. I remember seeing the burger place sign, but I don't recall them. I just ... it's residential over there …" She pointed. "But this whole area is. I just wish I could pin point where …"

Suddenly another tremor hit, this one stronger and longer. Enough to sway and knock both of them off the concrete.

Before they could get up, a huge 'boom' rocked the ground.

CJ saw it, not far ahead and a little to the right, a huge fireball shot to the sky. It appeared to reach for the clouds then quickly retracted, leaving behind a shadow of thick smoke. "Holy shit."

"Oh!" Mindy said brightly. "I figured it out." She pointed to the map.

"How do you know this all of the sudden?"

"That." She indicted to the smoke in the sky. "That was this gas station. It exploded. Now we know where we are."

NINE

He was a person who believed the worst of situations could bring out the best in people. Guy was not let down.

He was gathering up his strength, holding onto Carter, preparing to walk … somewhere, when a family walking through the rubble approached.

It looked like a family. A mother, father and teenage son.

"You need some help?" the father asked.

"Oh my goodness." The woman rushed over to Carter. "What happened?"

Guy peered at her, she had open gashes on her face, and looked in need of medical attention herself.

"We got caught in the wave. He had drown. Just ... I don't know where we are and I need to get him some help."

"We're trying to find it ourselves," she said. "Kep," she looked at her husband. "Do we have anything dry we can put on this boy?"

"I'll look." He slid a bag from his shoulder.

"I have a t-shirt," the teenage boy said, "He can have that."

"He needs to be warm," the woman said.

"Are you folks just walking?" asked Guy. "Or do you know where you want to be?"

"Walking," Kep answered. "Nothing is left around here. Hoping to get further east and find help for Mary."

"Honey," Mary knelt down to Carter and helped him change his shirt. "Do you think you can walk?" Carter nodded and she turned her head to Kep. "Give me a bottle of water. We need to keep him hydrated." When he gave her one, she extended it to Carter. "Take a drink. There you go."

Instantly, it seemed the woman mothered him, and Guy journeyed with them. While he needed to know how his own son was doing, his priority at that moment was Carter.

Kep and his teenage son helped Guy carry Carter. He and Carter were strangers to this family, yet they reached out to him.

They traveled together, walking at a slow pace. Most of the homes appeared modest and to be single story, they were leveled like card houses.

Kep stated several times he had lost his sense of direction, and he kept trying desperately to find a landmark.

The family was home having lunch when the earthquake hit, or whatever it was that shook the foundation of not only buildings but lives.

For all Guy knew they could have been heading north or south. He just wished there was a way to leave a message for CJ, to help find him.

Kep and Mary told him his best bet was to find a public shelter or emergency center and then try to find CJ.

Finally, not long into their walk the sounds of distant gunfire, explosions, rumbling ground and people crying were no longer the only sounds. Sirens rang out and helicopters could also be heard.

'Emerging from the ashes,' Guy thought, then said, "It's about time." And looked up to the sky when a helicopter flew by. "Anyone know how long it's been? You know, since this happened?"

Kep tapped his watch a few times. "Looks like just about three hours ago."

"My God. Three hours?" Guy asked.

"Closer to four, I bet," Mary added. "Looking to the sky. "It has to be near six. Your watch keeps stopping."

"Yeah, it does." Kep held it to his ear.

"I can't believe it has taken that long to hear some sirens," Guy said.

"They'll only come out if they can help," Kep said. "I think we should stop. Take a break. Pull out those energy bars for the kids."

Mary nodded. As she slipped the bag from her shoulder she paused at the sound of a rumbling motor and air brakes.

A huge, orange colored, county truck stopped right behind them.

Humanity strikes again.

"Any of you folks need some medical attention?" the driver asked, then stepped out.

"Yes," Mary answered. "The boy does. He had drown, and I have these …" she pointed to her face.

"I'm making a run to the elementary school," the driver said. "They're getting an emergency center together there. I'll take the injured if you'd like a ride. If you aren't injured, I can't take you. I need the room in the back."

Mary faced Guy. "Take Carter in the truck." She handed him a protein bar. "You need to get him seen by a medical person."

"You need to be seen as well."

"I won't leave my family."

"Mary," Kep said. "Go. Me and George will walk. We can make it. We'll follow behind in the truck."

"I don't want to leave you."

"Go. We won't be far behind. I promise."

Mary agreed and walked to the back of the truck with Guy.

When the driver pulled down the hatch, Guy was shocked to see the number of people in the back of the truck. They were all injured, some really bloody. All in some sort of shell shock state. Guy, Mary and Carter climbed inside. They sat near the back, on the bed of the county maintenance truck. Guy sat near the gate looking out as Kep and George followed.

They moved slowly, driving over rubble. Guy knew Kep and his son George wouldn't have a problem trailing the truck. It couldn't move very fast.

Even at a slow pace, the truck was taking them farther away, and each block they traveled added to the impossibility of Guy reuniting with his own son any time soon.

The water finally ended and with it was the painful reality of how much death and destruction the wave brought. CJ and Mindy had walked the edge of the water the entire distance, and in doing so didn't register how wide the water had spread.

The wave moved inland unevenly, some spots deeper, and CJ supposed some spots were barely hit. He knew for a fact that the collapsing of 105 caused almost a funnel for the water, creating almost a river.

Though the water had receded where they now walked, it was evident it had been washed over.

But the river was wide, wider than even CJ originally thought. He didn't think of it like the ocean sweeping in, had he done so he would not have been emotionally prepared.

Bodies.

When they arrived at completely dry land, untouched by water or the wave, all they saw were bodies.

Too many to count, too many to truly see them all.

There had to be thousands, if not tens of thousands.

They ventured off the path of 105 into a mostly residential area. The houses were crumbled, mere shells of themselves, and the bodies were everywhere. Any flat area, they were there … on top of rubble, against cars, in cars.

Left to right, as far as he could see. Death.

The wave had been humongous, it came in like the monster it was. As if it were the being from the movie, 'The Blob', collecting everything and anything in its path, only to spit whatever it collected out when it was finished.

CJ cringed, it reminded him of the pictures he had seen from the massive Indonesian Tsunami and the bodies on the beach.

Or a playing field for a massive rock concert where everyone just dropped dead.

The people who lost their lives didn't just drop dead, they lived long enough to know what was happening to them, to be scared, to cry and pray.

It was heart wrenching, even more so to think that his father and son could be out there among them.

The only way for CJ to know was to look, and he would. He and Mindy would look at every single body even if it took all night.

He had to. It was the only way to know, and until he did, he couldn't move forward.

TEN

The orange of flames dotted throughout the area. The people around them were mere shadows. The campfires were their only source of light. The sky was partly cloudy, making the night sky even darker, sporadically blocking out the stars and moon.

Despite his pain, Ruben could have kept going. But fate had other plans, or rather, those in authority had other plans. As the sun faded, and the temperature dropped, Roger tried to make a fire for those they had pulled from the water and wreckage.

There was a woman there, Ruben had wished he had gotten her name. She searched cars, finding water and things they could use for bandages and blankets, along with other items. One of which was the note he would eventually leave for CJ when they had to leave.

The large military truck rolled by just after six pm.

The truck and the four men in it took most of the people that Ruben had gathered and said they'd be back.

A curfew was being placed in effect.

"Do we know what happened?" Ruben asked. "Is it all of Los Angeles?"

No one gave him answers, just said they would be back.

"To take us where?" Ruben asked. "Do you know where? We have people out there searching, they're supposed to be back. We have to let them know where."

"We'll head to station four," the man told him. "It's 104 and Crenshaw."

"Is that where we'll go?"

"More than likely."

Ruben wrote that information down on some hotel stationary the woman had found and he placed the note in the door jamb of the limo, hoping that Mindy and CJ would return and find it.

They hadn't returned yet.

Ruben wasn't worried. He figured the late hour and the

darkness caused them to stop.

Three hours later the truck did return. At that point Ruben was hungry and thirsty, his fingers and thumb were numb and his arm had swollen to the point it didn't look like his own limb. He and Roger loaded into the back of the truck and began the next leg of their adventure.

He didn't realize how flat the area was until he saw how leveled everything was. There wasn't a whole building in sight. Nothing remotely recognizable remained.

The truck moved slowly, bouncing as it crossed over debris.

They were headed to a camp somewhere. How an address was even established, Ruben didn't know. Perhaps they were at the epicenter of the quake and the farther out they traveled the less damage there would be.

There had to be something remaining or how else would they be able to organize rescue workers?

Ruben just watched from the back of the truck, cradling his arm.

The first thing he wanted to do when he got to wherever they were going was to see if they had a phone or some sort of communication. He thought about his son and how worried he and his father had to be. He just wanted to get word to him that he was alright.

When they finally arrived to their destination, the truck stopped and one of the rescue workers came around to the back and opened the gate. Then he just walked away.

He said nothing, he didn't tell anyone what to do or where to go.

When Ruben unloaded from the truck he looked around. He couldn't tell where they were, or what sort of place it was. It looked like a massive campsite or compound. Large campfires had been built, and multitudes of people surrounded them. Echoing voices called out in the darkness as if coming from some sort of megaphone. Multitudes of tents had been erected and one small square brick structure remained.

There appeared to be no organization. It was chaos. However, there were people … life.

Right then and there his end of the world, neurotic fears had been relieved. It was bad, but it wasn't the apocalypse.

It was a localized disaster, plain and simple, something they'd make it through. There was help. It wasn't as bad as he originally feared

At least, that was what Ruben thought.

Guy had fallen asleep. In a chair next to Carter he rested his elbow on Carter's cot, propped his face in his hand and fell asleep. He was able to relax. They had arrived in the camp hours earlier and nothing was really there. It was still in the building stages.

Trucks with supplies moved in. Ill were separate from the healthy. Anyone with medical training was there to assist, but they had no tools, no real means to help.

Then just after sunset things started to take hold.

More trucks arrived with supplies. The Red Cross showed up. Guy and the others were the first to arrive and got the most attention.

Guy didn't know what was happening after Carter was seen by a doctor, and he really didn't care. His grandson's wellbeing was first and foremost.

The doctor that attended to Carter told Guy that the child was lucky. Most drowning victims in the wave didn't survive. Even though he had fluid in his lungs, he would recover with rest. Carter was placed on a cot in a tent with other people. People with cuts, bruises and head injuries. Guy stayed by his side. He was asked if he needed medical attention, but Guy felt his injuries, while sore, were minor.

He was told there was food and a warm beverage, but Guy didn't care about that. He didn't want to leave Carter. He watched as the tent filled to capacity. There were no longer enough cots for the inured or ill, only spaces on the floor.

In a folding chair, next to the cot, Guy stayed holding his grandson's hand, grateful he'd be okay and worried about CJ.

Then Guy relaxed enough to fall asleep.

He slept hard, long and deep, even in an uncomfortable position until he was awakened by another aftershock. It wasn't the quaking ground that stirred him from his slumber. It was the eruption of screams.

It had to be the hundredth one Guy felt, and people still screamed in fear. Even Guy was shaken by it, taking an immediate hovering and protective stance over Carter until it subsided.

But this one jolted him awake. Carter slept peacefully, attached to an IV and propped up on pillows.

Guy could hear noise outside the tent. Trucks, voices, someone speaking over a PA.

His stomach rolled in hunger and his mouth was dry. It was time to seek out that food table, or at least get a beverage.

He walked through the medical tent, looking at each and every person he passed, just in case CJ was there. There was a female nurse at a table by the tent entrance. She was writing things down, looking through clipboards. Guy asked her about food and she told him a table was set up center of the camp, he couldn't miss it.

Once outside, Guy froze. When he arrived there weren't that many people. Now, it was a massive endeavor. As far as they eye could see there were refugees from the disaster. They gathered around campfires, laying on the ground. More tents had been erected, big ones, like the medical tent he had just walked from. It went from a miniscule attempt being an aid station to a massive chaotic endeavor. There wasn't a spot of open area to be seen.

In the distance emergency spotlights were erected. Guy used them as his beacon and headed that way, dodging trucks that rolled by, bringing more people.

He tied to keep his wits about him, remembering where he

walked, looking back every few feet. He didn't want to get lost or lose his sense of direction and not be able to find Carter.

Soon he found the food table. A canteen was set up. It had a long line. A self-serve, giant coffee urn before a couple of tired workers served up soup and bread.

Guy waited in line. He was hungry. Carter was sleeping, now he could get his food and coffee and return to the child before he woke up.

No one spoke to each other, not at all. Everyone was shell shocked, moving about aimlessly, inching forward, no expression, almost like zombies.

As he waited in line Guy did notice one thing. A man. He sat off to the side of the table on the ground, and he held a radio to his ear.

Guy kept watching him. His eyes shifting to the man, not wanting to lose him.

Just as he was given his bowl of soup Guy heard the call of his name.

"Mr. James. Hey, Mr. James."

Cup and tray of food in hand, Guy turned. Sure enough he recognized the man.

His entire arm was in a cast and the man rushed to Guy. It was the limousine driver.

"Oh my God," the man said. "You're alive."

Guy just stared at him.

"Ruben. I'm Ruben," he said. "Mindy's …"

"Yes. Yes. I know. You were trapped in the Humvee," Guy replied.

"Roger got me out."

"My son … his son had gone down to help him. Have you seen him?"

"He's fine," Ruben said.

Guy exhaled with a gasp of relief. "Is he here?"

"No. He went looking for you and his son. Is the boy … is your grandson …"

"Fine. Alive." Guy replied. "He's okay. He's resting. Healing, but fine."

"That's good to hear."

"But my kid's alright, correct?" Guy asked. "He's fine?"

"Yes. And I left word of where they were taking us."

Guy felt the weight of the world drop from him and he wanted to scream in relief. His child was alive and well. Even though he wasn't there, he was alright. And that was music to Guy's ears.

"I have no doubt," Ruben said. "He should be here by morning or at least afternoon."

"I can't tell you how relieved that makes …" Guy paused when the man holding the radio walked back to the food line.

"You alright?" Ruben asked.

"Yes, just … excuse me." Guy walked away from Ruben to the man that held the small radio to his ear.

Ruben followed.

The man refilled his coffee.

"Excuse me," Guy stopped him. "Excuse me."

The man turned to him. "Yes?"

"You have that radio, are you getting anything?" Guy asked.

"Some."

"Any news? Do you know what happened?"

"Not much detail," the man replied. "I just know it's bad everywhere."

"So the entire Los Angeles area is bad?" Guy questioned.

"No. Not only Los Angeles. It looks like everywhere," the man said. "I mean … everywhere."

ELEVEN

CJ threw up.

It was a combination of the head injury and the countless bodies that surrounded him. It was a daunting task, some he didn't need to look at. He skipped over the women at first and then he felt guilty because there they were, they died alone. No one to hold their hand, to watch them take their last breath. Simply acknowledging them was the least CJ could do. He couldn't cover them, give them any final moments of dignity. The only kindness he could show was to move them together so they weren't just scattered bodies, bent and twisted over rock and rubble.

He and Mindy moved them as best they could, clearing out a huge section, but barely making a dent.

Then it got too dark to see, so they stopped.

"Here's some more dry wood," Mindy added it to the fire. "Did you want to go back?"

"No." CJ shook his head. "We have to look. My father and son were swept away. Chances are …" he glanced outward. "They're here."

"I'm sorry."

"Yeah, me, too."

"Pop-Tart?" she asked brightly as she sat down.

"Excuse me?"

"Pop-Tart." She extended the rectangular pastry to him. "I had them in my bag. I'll look for more food if you want something more substantial."

"This … this will work, thank you." He broke it in half after taking it and then had a small nibble. "So you brought Pop-Tarts, you found wood, a lighter, water and ibuprofen. That's pretty impressive."

"The world is a treasure chest, you just need to know where to dig."

"And how does a rich pop star know this?" he asked.

"Rich, aging popstar," she smiled. "The average age of my fan base is in their late thirties. I know how to find the treasures because when I was little my mother and I were homeless."

"I never knew that. Not that I know much about you."

"We didn't let that information out. My mother was a very proud woman. She never wanted people to know. But … I learned a lot."

"Yeah, obviously."

"One thing I did learn was this right here, where we are, isn't going to work for rest. We need to find shelter."

CJ huffed out a laugh in ridicule. "Where? Everything was flattened."

"Right here it was flattened, but if we walk we can find somewhere where it wasn't."

"If we walk … we won't be able to finish what we start."

"You mean searching the bodies?"

CJ nodded.

"Do you really think they're gone? That they're … well … passed away?"

"I don't know."

"If you don't know, CJ, why are you focusing on the negative? Searching the bodies is confirming they are dead. I would rather try to find them alive."

"How do we do that?"

"Not sitting in a sea of death. I am positive there has to be sets ups or camps, there has to be. There are plans in order for disasters like this. We need to find them, they won't find us." She reached into a bag. "I have this handy dandy roadside assistance flashlight and red rescue light all in one. Let's start walking."

"Where did you get …" CJ waved out his hand. "Never mind, you found it. Right?"

"I did. It will be enough light for us to walk. And the sky …" She peered up. "Is clearing so that will also help light the way."

"What are we looking for?"

"Life. People. We'll ask. But life and people are not here."

"You're right. We can't just sit here until we can see." He stood.

"Then let's go." She pulled out her phone.

"Still searching for a signal?"

"No. I have a little battery power left. I'm using the compass. We need to head northeast, toward LA. Maybe we will find camps along the way."

"Thanks for coming with me." As soon as he said that the ground rumbled for a few seconds. CJ paused, closed his eyes and shook his head. "I'll never get used to this."

"I don't think anyone does."

"Feels like the world is falling apart. But … I know that isn't what's happening, right?"

"It would take an awful big event to make the world fall apart."

"And an earthquake isn't …" CJ stopped. Suddenly he felt the pressure in his ears. It went from that to a buzzing sound, and the air around him seemed to ripple. "Shit."

"What the heck?" Mindy placed her palm flat to her ear.

"It's happening again."

And as he suspected, as soon as those words slipped from his mouth, the recognizable boom rang out. Only again, like on the highway, CJ lifted his head to the sky. Remnants of what looked like a donut shaped fireball marked the sky and changed to smoke as a blue and orange streak of light sailed across the sky.

"I'd say we should run," she looked at CJ. "But there's nowhere … to run to."

In a shocked whisper, CJ replied. "Brace for impact."

TWELVE

Ruben saw three. They were undeniable and streaked across the sky seconds after they entered into earth's atmosphere with a loud explosion. Scientifically it didn't make sense, usually the sound occurred when an object crossed the barrier of sound. But meteorites traveled faster than the speed of sound at seven hundred and sixty-seven miles per miles.

Perhaps it was nothing more than nature's warning. But they moved fast and Ruben could only guess they were three of many. Many that had come and many more to arrive.

There was no official report to confirm that.

It was him logically putting things together.

CJ told Roger he swore he saw something in the sky, and that was after the first quake. Then shortly after came the wave ... was it an ocean hit or an earthquake somewhere else?

Joel was the man with the handheld radio. He kept winding it up to keep the power. A self-proclaimed prepper, Ruben wondered what he was doing in Los Angeles. Usually those prepper types lived far from the city. Was he traveling?

"First vacation I had in twelve years," Joel told him. "I live in the hills. I was on my way to LAX when I got a text from a friend. I tried to find it on the news on the radio, but nothing. Sure enough everything east of Oklahoma shut off from the world."

That was his response when Ruben questioned him on how he knew what was going on.

Now the transistor type radio was picking up broken news casts and snippets of radio broadcast from amateurs

When he first met Joel in the canteen line, Joel told him the earth was being pelted by a series of meteorites and asteroids, all raining down, and they expected it to continue for twenty-four hours. Last he heard the east was hit pretty bad, too.

It wasn't going to end there.

Perhaps it was him not wanting to believe it that caused Ruben to walk away and label the man a little insane, but once Guy fell asleep next to his grandson, Ruben left to find Roger and came across Joel again.

Joel was an instant celebrity in the camp. Seated just outside the school's large tool shed, which was now being used as the main canteen, he was encircled by a group of people around a fire, Joel told how it was ironic that he had prepared for every disaster, even had a stockpile at his house and in his car. Not only was he not at home when the big one hit, his car was crushed and then washed away. There he was, without anything. But he was going to make it home, of that he was certain.

He answered questions on what people could do, gave his theories on what was happening.

"If hundreds of those things fly from the sky," Joel said. "It's like being hit with hundreds of bombs a thousand times stronger than Hiroshima. To make matters worse, who knows what chain of events they could unleash, if they haven't already."

Ruben wasn't prepared to buy into Joel, the apocalypse prophet, so he made his way over to Roger.

"You listening to this?" Ruben asked.

"It's interesting. What else is there to do?" Roger replied.

Then it happened.

The weird sensation felt in the air and the loud 'boom'. Ruben glanced to the sky. They sailed across like jets in a fighter formation. It was hard to tell which was larger, because one of the three could have been lower.

He just knew it wasn't going to be long before he felt the impact of at least one of them.

Ruben was right.

It was as if the ground exploded. It shook violently, immediately cracking the concrete, lifting it high and ejecting people upwards.

It didn't stop.

It wasn't just a quake, it was rocking up, down, left and right, so loud it drowned out the screaming. Then came the winds.

It could have been a nuclear warhead for all they knew because it seemed to follow the same effect.

Ruben heard them coming, a deep roar and had it not been night, he probably wouldn't have seen them. He merely caught a glimpse, a second before it felt as if he were blasted by a wall. Ruben and the others were already at a disadvantage. Their footing was unstable as they tried to remain upright from the quake. When the blast wind arrived it knocked into Ruben, sending him sailing through the air.

There was no fighting it, no stopping it, Ruben just prayed.

Guy was asleep when the earth shook so hard it knocked him from his chair and bounced him twice from the ground, upward like a rubber ball. Immediately, as soon as he could stand he dove for Carter. He yanked out the IV, lifted the boy, held him close to his chest and focused on protecting him and getting him out.

But to go where?

Patients in the medical tent rolled to the floor, their cots falling on them. The sturdy tent waved and rippled as nature created an obstacle course for Guy to cross. Fallen injured, cots tumbling. Guy did his best to make his way through, but it wasn't enough.

There was nothing sturdy to hide under, no doorframe to take cover.

He was certain this wasn't any ordinary disaster, or the recent tremor after tremor following the quakes weren't aftershocks.

Then again, Guy didn't know much about earthquakes at all. It was all pure guessing.

He barely made it halfway across the medical tent when he heard the deep rumbling of destruction. Focusing forward, Guy never saw the back end of the tent whip out from the posts that held it down.

Like the gathering of a table cloth with all contents on it, the tent whirled around, grabbing everything into it, lifting them from the ground and carried them so fast, Guy felt as if he were on some sort of ride. He didn't tumble, he was part of everything else, just moving them wherever the wind decided.

Closing his eyes, he held tight to Carter bracing for the inevitable landing. One he feared would shake the child from his hold.

It wasn't as brutal as he thought, the bunched tent landed on the ground and moved across the surface with fast momentum until it slowed down and finally stopped.

Safe. He was safe, and they weren't even hurt.

He actually laughed in gratitude, hugging Carter. Although they were twisted in the tent, they had made it. They just had to get out.

The ground shook again, just a tremor, but it was enough to tell him that not everyone had survived the whirlwind.

There were no cries and no screams, just a few distant moans and sobs.

The fabric of the tent was just above his head and Guy attempted to stand. He stumbled some and looked around, trying to find a way out of the tangled mess.

He pushed against the fabric trying to find the end.

Not only was Carter heavy, but the tent was heavy against him as well. The weight and darkness made moving difficult.

As if a guiding light of salvation beckoned an orange hue took over the tent, and it enabled Guy to spot the small plastic window of the tent. It was ten feet from him. He'd make it, he was sure. He trudged over toward that small opening, he needed to rip the plastic window open if he wanted to get out from the canvas.

Nearly there, Guy searched the items he stepped over. He needed something to break through the plastic if it didn't have an opening or zipper. Then his foot caught it. It was a lamp. Not a normal lamp, but a bendable metal floor lamp, one of several that had been positions between the cots. Guy reached down and grabbed it as he arrived at the plastic squared window.

"I have to put you down," he told Carter.

Carter nodded.

"Hang on to Pap's leg."

"Okay."

Guy examined the plastic window, looking and feeling for a seal or opening. A zipper even. Nothing.

He grabbed the lamp, the lightbulb was broken and he tried to use that to cut the plastic. The problem was there wasn't much room for momentum. The tent rested against his head and the window was at his chest level.

It wasn't working.

He turned the lamp upside down.

"Pap."

"One second." Guy unscrewed the base, exposing the open pipe like the end of the lamp. Using that end he pushed it against the plastic,

"Pap!" Carter cried out.

Then he coughed.

It was at that moment Guy realized he himself had been coughing, he had just been too focused to even pay attention.

He peered over his shoulder and his eyes widened in fear. The entire back end of the tent was engulfed in flames.

He had seconds, if that, before escape wouldn't be possible.

"Cover your mouth," he told Carter as he pulled him near him. Guy pushed with everything he had against the plastic window. It wouldn't poke through.

"Come on!" He urged and pleaded as he gave it all he had.

The heat in the tent increased, and not only was it deadly, it worked in his favor. The end of the lamp poked through the softening plastic.

Guy yanked out the pole, then using all of his strength he placed his fingers in the hole and using both hands, pulled back and ripped.

"Pap!" Carter screamed.

Guy whisked him upward and feet first, shoved Carter through the opening.

The heavy tent lessened in weight as most of it disappeared, engulfed in flames.

Guy could barely breathe. The smoke was all encompassing and debilitating. He coughed and choked, but he didn't look back. He knew it was close. The opening widened as the rest of the plastic peeled away and Guy protruded through the window head first.

He gasped in the fresh air and saw Carter standing there.

The little boy held out his hand and Guy, twisting and turning to get through, freed himself just as the flames arrived.

He charged forth, grabbed on to Carter and backed away. After lifting him into his arms again, he cradled him close covering his eyes and ears, protecting him not only from the sight of the fire, but the screams of agony that came from the tent as the remaining survivors in there were burned alive.

THIRTEEN

'I'm not surviving this. I'm not surviving this,' CJ thought the second he felt the ground erupt. "I've been thrown around, almost drowned and my head cracked … this is it. This is the end.'

His saving grace was there were no standing structures. Nothing to fall on him. His threat was the buckling earth that lifted up at least ten feet in some areas. He smacked against a wall of earth before tumbling down and laying in a semi-conscious state until it was all over with.

Eventually the ground stopped shaking and whatever kind of blast wind that hit him, ceased.

He was laying on his side and he rolled over, then knelt. He felt his chest and head, searching for injuries. He didn't feel anything, but adrenaline could have masked the pain.

He was fine. He was alive. He stared down to his hand and was able to see himself.

How long had he been out? Long enough for the sun to rise? The area was lit with a beautiful pre-sunrise lighting.

As he basked in his gratefulness, it hit him.

Mindy.

He took a deep breath and shouted. "Mindy!"

His voice didn't echo, it was muffled by the wall of dirt behind him.

"Mindy!"

"CJ."

He heard her and he stood. "Mindy."

"Where are you?"

"Everything looks the same. There's some sort of wall." He moved. "The ground lifted."

"I see that."

"Keep talking. I think I see you."

CJ looked left to right. "I'm talking. I'm talking. I'm can't see you." What he did see was the cracked ground, lifted and split.

"No … that's not you. It's a body."

He rolled his eyes. "Swell. Are you hurt?"

"No."

"Start singing. I'll come to you."

"CJ, I really don't feel like singing."

"Just sing."

"Fine."

Mindy did.

It was that point he realized that maybe all those rumors about her being 'auto tuned; were true. The singing was horrendous and out of tune. But it could have been tiredness or their situation.

Finally he saw her, she stood about thirty feet from him. Had the sky not started to lighten he probably wouldn't have seen her at all.

He raced her way and like old friends, they embraced.

"You're alright." He grabbed hold of her arms looking at her.

"Yes, you?"

"I'm fine. I don't know how."

"I have never felt that. I have felt earthquakes before. That had to be the strongest quake. But that wind …"

"It was a meteor or asteroid. That was the blast wave. Like a bomb. I saw it. In the sky."

"Like the one with the dinosaurs?"

"God, I hope not. That one set the planet on fire."

"Do you think it was another meteor that started this?"

"I do. I saw one earlier and no one believed me. We need to keep moving. I don't know how safe it is here."

Mindy nodded and reached down for her bag.

"Wait. You still have your bag."

"I had it strapped to me, but took it off because I got scratched." She lifted her shirt. The gash was deep and bleeding.

"Holy shit. Give me the bag." He took it and opened it, reaching inside and feeling around. Once he felt something cloth like, he pulled it out. It was a sweater. "Hold this against your stomach. We have to get you help."

"It doesn't hurt."

"I'm sure it will. That's bad." He shouldered the bag for her.

"It's just a scratch. Really. Your head wound is worse."

"Not really."

"Yeah, it is."

"Can we not compare injuries?" He took hold of her arm. "Let's just keep moving."

"I'm glad we are walking together."

"You realize I am the worst person you can be with right?" CJ asked.

"Why do you say that?"

"I have absolutely no survival skills whatsoever."

"I wouldn't say that."

The walked, moving slowly as they cautiously stepped over rocks and other debris.

"How long were you looking for me?" CJ asked.

"Not long. A second. Why?'

"So you were knocked out, too?"

"No. Not at all. Everything stopped and I stood. Then I heard you call."

"We had to be knocked out. The sun is up and it was night …" his words slowed down and he stopped walking.

"What?"

CJ, fearfully looked over his shoulder. "Oh my God."

"What's wrong? Did …" Mindy gasped in shock.

CJ couldn't move and he couldn't look away.

The sun hadn't risen. Daylight wasn't what caused the brightness.

The entire horizon was lit up orange and yellow. It was as if the entire sky … was on fire.

"Holy Mother of God," Ruben recited the phrase then closed his eyes. The first thing he saw upon standing up was the skyline ablaze.

After taking a second, he stumbled forward looking at it.

It looked as if the sun exploded, lighting every bit of the atmosphere on fire.

He knew it had to be moving his way, slowly and tauntingly.

He wasn't a big science guy, but knew enough and watched enough online videos to know that when an asteroid impacted the earth it created a fireball.

Three of them had sailed across the sky.

The ground shook from their impact, and the blast wave knocked him over.

The fireball ignited the sky and he knew it would only spread.

It was still the middle of the night, that much he knew, yet it looked bright enough to be dawn.

After getting over the shock of the sky, Ruben faced the shock of his surroundings.

The entire camp was flattened. Fires blazed all around. The tents were gone and the school shed used as a canteen was flattened. Bits and pieces of it strewn about. A small fire raged where the canteen once was. The two story school which had survived the original quake had collapsed in the middle. The stadium could no longer be seen.

There were very little sounds, people calling out names, crying, shouting for help and occasionally the sound of an explosion in the distance.

The world had fallen apart.

Other than a few scratches, bumps and bruises on his body Ruben was fine. Those around him were not.

He saw legs and arms outstretched from under the rubble, but no one moved. It happened so fast. One second he was standing next to Roger and the next …

Roger.

He was standing next to Roger.

Ruben spun around, running back to where he had landed. He and Roger were not the only ones. There were a lot of people in that area. Joel and his engaged fan club encircled a fire that had been extinguished by the blast.

Ruben couldn't be the only one alive,

"Anyone alive?" Ruben called out. "Anyone hurt?"

No one replied.

It couldn't be. There was no way no one else survived.

"Anyone!" Ruben shouted louder. He then began the task of looking and checking everybody he could find.

He saw an arm, the finger nails painted some shade of blue and Ruben bent down to feel for the wrist.

There wasn't a pulse.

He sighed out. As he stood he paused when he saw it.

That yellow emergency, wind up transistor radio of Joel's. It was on the ground. Unscathed. Untouched.

He lifted the heavy object, wound it a few times and turned on the knob.

Static.

It worked.

He placed it in his back pocket and continued his search. Lifting pieces of metal and wood, Ruben continuously called out, "Hello! Anyone. Roger!"

Every single body he spotted, he checked.

How? How was he the only one to make it?

In the distance he heard voices, and shouting.

Maybe Roger was thrown farther. Perhaps he had to move away from where he was. Just because he ended up there didn't mean that Roger did.

He kept calling his name, calling for anyone as he moved on.

"Ruben?"

Ruben halted in his search,

The voice was tired and raspy.

"Ruben!"

Ruben turned toward the call of his name and his shoulders dropped in relief.

Guy stood twenty or so feet away. There was no mistaking him. He stood next to Carter and they waved.

They made it. They were alive.

Ruben wasn't alone.

FOURTEEN

"Why are you crying, Pap? Why are you crying? What's wrong?" Carter asked, tugging on Guy's pant leg.

Guy had broken.

Just after he had made the narrow escape from the tent, he watched seconds later as everything was engulfed by the fire, Guy stumbled backwards, sat down and cried. Something he hadn't done in years. Even when his wife died after a long illness, Guy barely shed a tear. Yet, right there and then Guy lost it.

They had made it. When they did and he knew they were safe, he had reached his emotional end. Every bit of him was spent both physically and emotionally.

Guy had no other recourse but to stop, sit down and mentally break.

He hated that he did so in front of Carter. He simply could not go on until he stopped.

"I'm okay. It's okay." Guy told Carter.

"But why are you crying? Are you hurt?"

"No. No. I'm okay. Are you?" Guy hugged him.

"Yeah. Where's my dad?"

"I don't know. I wish I did."

Guy believed he and Carter were alone. A few seconds after his meltdown and he had gotten himself together, Guy stood up and saw Ruben.

Ruben was searching. Lifting items and looking underneath, and that was when Guy realized that Roger wasn't around.

They had their reunion, then after Guy found Carter a safe place to sit, they searched together.

Sadly, Joel, the radio and prepper guy didn't make it. He was crushed beneath the debris from the shed. How awful it was, Guy thought. There he was, a man prepared for the end of the world, only to be taken out in the snap of a finger.

The search for Roger didn't take long.

The man who was on the pop star's security force, the one that got Guy and CJ on the shuttle … sadly, didn't make it.

When they found him a good fifteen yards from where Ruben was last with him, Roger was curled up on his side looking as if he were sleeping.

He was one of many.

So many of the hundreds at that camp didn't make it.

There was a sense of sadness and defeat. Drowning in their feelings until they found a clearing and stopped for the next few hours.

When the real light of day appeared things seemed less dismal.

The burning sky in the distance didn't look as menacing as it did at night, and more people had emerged from the rubble. They were gathering, looking for food and water, all of them moving in some sort of slow pilgrimage after the sun had risen.

However, even though the enflamed horizon didn't seem threatening, Guy knew that it was. The only option the survivors had was to walk away from it. And that was the only plan.

A group of people that remained from the camp, thirty or forty strong, meandered their way across the destruction. No real place to go, and no knowledge of what was ahead.

The need to get Carter to safety agonizingly outweighed the need to go back and search for his son.

Guy hoped and prayed that the world normalized soon. They would eventually happen upon help. Though it wasn't anywhere in sight, it had to be out there somewhere.

He had seen enough natural disasters on television. The news showed the military always moving out to the affected areas. This Guy believed would be no different.

They had been walking amongst the others for hours, no real direction at all, just east. Away from the burning sky. The temperature felt like it surpassed a hundred degrees.

Things were looking up some, finally two large dump trucks

rolled by stopping to pick up the survivors.

Thoughts of a catastrophic event that wiped out the world slowly left his mind. After all, would trucks come to transport them if the world had moved into extinction mode?

It felt good to stop, to sit down. Even if it was on the floor bed of a cold metal truck, crammed in with dozens of other people. He, Ruben and Carter were able to stop walking, resting some, and that was a good thing.

Those in the truck were frightened. It was evident by the conversation strangers struck up.

"Anyone know where we're going?" someone asked.

"Or what is happening," another said.

"I saw a movie once," a young man, no older than twenty, spoke up. "Some sun event or meteor hit the earth. It caused a fireball. People in Australia had like twelve hours warning. That was what the movie was about. The last twelve hours before the world ended. I wonder if the red sky means that. Nowhere to go,"

"Do you mind?" Guy asked. "There's a kid here. I don't want to scare him."

"Sorry. I just … we're in a truck going somewhere, but is there anywhere really to go?"

"I'm sure it's not as bad as your movie. If you wouldn't mind not talking about it, I'd appreciate it."

"Sorry." The young man lowered his head.

"He's scared," Ruben whispered. "He doesn't mean anything by it. He's just talking. He needs to talk."

"I know," Guy replied. "I don't want Carter to hear or worry." Guy pulled his grandson closer. "He's been through enough. I don't …" Guy paused when the sound of helicopters grew louder. He exhaled. "Thank God. I was beginning to worry."

"That." Ruben pointed upward. "Is a good sign."

Guy agreed. He tugged Carter to him and smiled, but it was short lived. The smile quickly dropped from his face when a voice over a speaker came from the chopper.

"This is an evacuation area. You are advised to immediately move east. Please seek higher ground. Repeat, this is an evacuation area, you are advised to move east and to get to higher ground as quickly as possible."

The announcement continued, not changing infliction, not pausing. A continuous warning message as they flew off.

Guy listened to the announcement even as the helicopter moved onward, fading from earshot.

Evacuation.

Higher ground.

At that moment the truck jolted as it immediately picked up speed.

The danger or event was far from over.

They weren't just moving away from what burned in the sky, they were moving away quickly from something else. Something bigger. The need to get to higher ground told Guy it could only be one thing ... another wave. They were already miles inland, with the urgency of the evacuation, Guy had to wonder how big that wave was going to be.

FIFTEEN

The night before didn't unfold as brutally for CJ as he imagined when he and Mindy began their walk.

About two hours into their walk, an old truck passed them. It moved slowly as it bounced over debris. CJ didn't even bother to wave, but the truck stopped anyways.

At first he believed it was a Good Samaritan move, until the young man in the passenger's seat yelled out, "hey, are you Mindy Snow?"

"I am," she replied. "Do I know you? Oh, are you one of my dancers?"

When CJ heard her ask that, he felt optimistic.

Then the young man replied, "I'm a fan. Do you need a ride somewhere?"

Mindy hobbled to the passenger side, explaining their quest.

The father and son team in the truck were on a similar one. They were headed home, trying to see if their family was alright.

"We were on our way back from the Long Beach," the young man named Dallas said. "We got off the highway for food when it hit."

"It's amazing your truck survived," said CJ.

"It didn't," Dallas replied. "This is the second one we found. We're just trying to get home. We stopped at a make shift hospital the military had set up, my dad needed stiches."

"So the military is up and running?" CJ asked.

Dallas nodded. "Was. Trying. The last quake destroyed the place we were at. We headed out after that. Hop on in."

"Where are you headed?" Mindy asked.

"North. We live in South Park. We can drop you off somewhere. We should be passing Saint Francis Medical Center on the way. We can drop you there. You guys look worse for wear."

"We feel it," Mindy said, then looked at CJ. "Do you want to?"

CJ thought about it for a second. He needed to stop and take a break, stopping at a hospital would give him a chance to see if his father and son were there. "Yes, thank you."

Of course, there was room in the cab of the truck for Mindy, but CJ had to ride in the back end. He was fine with that. It gave him time to think and to watch the reddened sky as they drove farther away from it.

The ride to the hospital didn't take long, even though they moved slowly. However, any semblance of a working hospital or emergency set up at Saint Francis Hospital was gone. Perhaps at one time after the first quake they tried to keep things going, but there was mass confusion, small fires and people wandering aimlessly.

It was a mess.

One thing CJ noticed, the farther away from their starting point they got, the less complete devastation.

There were more partially standing buildings and the roads for the most part weren't completely destroyed.

"Not sure, we should leave them here. I don't think they're helping people," Dallas' father said. "We should head home. That's our best option. If mom's not there, we can head to Community."

"Do we have enough gas?"

"We should make it."

CJ listened to their exchange, stepping away to look around. It just seemed so hopeless.

"You okay?" Mindy walked up to him.

"No." CJ shook his head. "What are we doing? We are going farther away from where I left my son and father."

"There's no easy way to find them," Mindy replied, pointing to Dallas and his father. "Our best bet is to find a place that's communicating with other camps. Or the military. There has to be a way to check in. Somewhere out there, they are trying to help."

"Somewhere out where?" CJ asked. "I don't think we should keep going. We're going to get so far away, I'll never find them."

"CJ, we were in an earthquake. We may not have news or phones, but a hundred miles away they're watching on the news. We saw the helicopters. They're just waiting until it's safe to come in and help. Once they do, everyone will be reunited."

"You sound very confident."

"I am. I've been through several quakes. Most small, but one wasn't. I don't know how much of my career you know of, but ten years ago I was in Japan performing when that nine point hit. I thought the world was over. It just seemed that way. Everywhere around me was destruction. But within a day or two the trucks rolled in, the government sent help and I was able to go home."

"Thank you."

"We just need to find someplace that's like a center of operations."

"Or ..." CJ looked around. "A place still standing."

"I'm betting the farther in LA that we go the more we'll find working and active areas. It's the middle of the night, we're tired. We either keep moving or stop and find a safe place to hold up."

"Ready?" Dallas approached the pair. "We're gonna head north to our house. See if my mom and sister are there. If not, we'll try the nearest hospital. That's Dignity. Not sure how the roads are or even if we can there, but we'll try. My dad seems to think that if we keep going we may get to areas less hit."

Mindy faced CJ. "Do you want to go or stay?"

Almost with reluctance, CJ nodded. "We'll go. Thank you, Dallas, thank you very much."

They loaded back into the truck and journeyed north, closer to downtown Los Angeles. CJ dozed off several times in the back of the truck, waking to the see the brightening sky of daylight. The ominous red sky that was now to his right, didn't seem as bad.

Maybe it wasn't some massive fireball headed their way, perhaps it was something totally different.

It was amazing how things seemed less helpless in the light of day. At least for CJ it was. For Dallas and his father things took another turn.

The buildings of their neighborhood suffered significant damage and when they arrived close enough to their home they parked, unable to get through the destructions. Homes had collapsed, the street had lifted in some spots forming ramps. Neighbors camped out in yards. CJ and Mindy followed the father and son duo to their house.

When they arrived there wasn't much there. The front of the house had completely crumbled and the roof had collapsed inside.

Dallas and his father raced in and began sifting through in desperation.

CJ wanted to help, he felt he had to. But as they stepped inside to aid the sounds of low flying helicopters rang through, and shortly after their arrival came the repeated announcement that they were in an evacuation zone.

Evacuate.

Higher ground.

They flew in circles listing landmarks, miles away where transport would be available.

"Jesus," CJ said. "Where in the world around here is higher ground?"

"This has got to be a joke, right?" Mindy asked. "It has to be."

CJ chuckled in almost ridicule. "I don't think they're flying around saying that to mislead people."

"We're twenty miles inland," Mindy said. "How is that even possible?"

CJ shook his head when he saw Dallas and his father emerge.

"They aren't there," Dallas said. "No sign of them at all."

"What now?" CJ asked.

Dallas' father replied. "We're gonna try my sister's house, they may have gone there."

"Where's that?"

"West of here."

"West?" CJ nearly shrieked. "That's the wrong way."

"We have to find my mom and sister," Dallas said.

"What about the warning. The evacuation," CJ asked. "Getting to higher ground."

"I'm sorry. But unless you're coming with us," Dallas' father said. "You're on your own."

And within seconds, CJ and Mindy were.

Dallas and his father hurried away back towards the truck. CJ and Mindy were left in an unknown area with no sense of direction, no time limit and absolutely no way but on foot to get to higher ground ... wherever that would be.

SIXTEEN

The White House – Washington, D.C.

FLASHBACK - 24 HOURS EARLIER ... Pre-Impact

There are presidents that are destined for greatness. Destined to have history remember them as political figures who made a positive difference in the life of those they served. There are presidents who fail, where history would remember them as those whose actions where harmful, useless and damaging. Those presidents were remembered for the good and the bad, students would instantly recognize their faces.

Then there were those like President Parker Wesley. Who seemingly would never make a mark on history, good or bad. Their faces, their names, buried beneath the one who were well known. Their names and presidency, a head scratcher to school children.

Parker believed he wanted to be president of the United States. He served as the youngest mayor of the city of Akron, on a whim, he joined the race. After killing it during the debates, there was no stopping the forty-four year old, single, handsome man.

He was motivated by the enthusiasm of the would-be voters, he rode the train of success, but two weeks prior to the elections he decided it wasn't for him.

He tried to pull out of the race, suggesting he give his nomination to the candidate of his party that came in second. But he was talked out of it, and decided to believe the polls that predicted he'd lose in a landslide loss.

He didn't.

He headed into office with the mindset that he would simply follow the footsteps and policies of his two-term predecessor, even though he was of a different party.

Lay low.

Get out.

Be the president no one would remember.

He had no idea he would be the last president of the United States.

Parker skated by. His cabinet handled almost everything and in the two years he had remaining, he looked forward to the elections, having announced he wouldn't run again.

He wasn't about to kill himself on the job, either. Not to say he didn't take it seriously, he did, but he wasn't out to change the world like so many before.

Parker wasn't expecting the world to change drastically on its own.

Unlike other presidents who enjoyed golf, Parker had two different hobbies. Building things and poker.

He'd head down to the local casino inconspicuously driving a Chevy Spark, sandwiched between a Subaru and minivan carrying a security detail. They pulled to the back and made their way to a private poker room. It wasn't high stakes, it was enough for him to be mindless, have a drink and smoke some cigars then hit his THC pen without being judged.

That was where he was when it all began.

Three times in his entire life of playing poker Parker was dealt a natural royal flush. The third and final time, poker face in full force, Parker had to fold when the his Chief of Staff came barreling in with the Secret Service, and without saying more than, 'you need to come with us', Parker was whisked away.

He didn't even get to drive his own Chevy Spark.

"Charles, what's happening?" Parker asked as soon as they were in the back of the SUV.

"Probably be easier to show you."

"Yeah, well, you can't pull a man from a natural royal flush and not explain why?"

"I understand. That glorious meteor shower that everyone's been talking about?"

"Yes?"

"Apparently the rocks coming off that asteroid belt aren't as small as we were led to believe."

"That means what?" Parker asked.

"It's not good."

"Explain not good."

"Instead of basketball size there are car size pieces that pretty much break apart as they enter. NASA is now confirming these objects range in size from one hundred feet to six hundred, massive. Most of them the same size as the one that flattened the area in Siberia in 1908."

"Jesus. How many will impact earth? Two or three?"

"Yes."

Parker nodded.

"Hundreds."

"What? My God."

"For the next forty-eight hours they will rain down."

"Where?"

"Everywhere. It's a crap shoot."

"How, Charles? How did we not see this coming? How did we not know their sizes?"

Charles shrugged. "Right now, Air Force One is being prepped to go. We need to get you inland in case of any Atlantic hits."

"Where to?"

"Cheyenne Mountain."

"Do our people think that's safe?" Parker asked.

"Our safest option," Charles answered. "Nowhere is really safe."

Air Force One

Nineteen Hours Earlier... Impact

For as many times as Parker had been on the Air Force One, he had never really been in the command room during a crisis. He visited during drills, but never really paid much attention and spoke only to say, 'great job'

He watched the airmen monitoring controls, military leaders barking out commands.

"Sir," an airman approached him. "We're preparing for landing. You may want to take your seat."

"Sure, thank you," Parker said and turned to leave.

"Sir," Charles called out. "We just lost the space station."

"What does that mean? They lost communications?" Parker asked. "Are they ..."

"Gone," Charles said. "Struck. Destroyed. Gone. The first of the rocks started making impact."

"Do we have a better idea where?"

"Fortunately it looks as if a good part of the first group is aiming for the Atlantic. Then as time ticks, the hits move west. From what they told me, it would be like spinning a globe slowly while you shoot darts at it, this trail of meteorites or super bolides is long. Thousands of miles."

"Dart guns, spinning globes. These are the analogies of our top minds?" Parker asked.

Charles lifted his shoulder and held out his hands in a 'who knows' manner, then simply responded, "Does it matter?"

"The Atlantic," Parker said. "What about those people on the shore?"

"There was not enough time to evacuate. We weren't sure where they would land."

"How?" Parked asked with edge. "How in God's name do we not have this information? Why is this a surprise? Someone had to of known."

"I'm sure some amateur star gazer may have thought it. But we didn't know it," Charles added. "NORAD or Cheyenne may have more information. We'll be landing …"

A bright blinding flash filled the plane, silencing everyone. Before the light faded, the plane jolted violently sending Parker up and back. That one jolt turned into several and the plane swayed drastically to the right as it quickly descended in altitude.

Parker was barely on his feet when he was grabbed and escorted to a seat. An oxygen mask dropped, he grabbed onto it as he was aided and strapped in.

The noise level of the struggling plane increased. His head spun, things happened so fast he didn't have time to process fear.

Charles took the seat next to him, placing on his belt.

"Are we going to crash?" Parker asked.

"I don't know," Charles replied. "Let's hope not."

Parker turned his head and looked out the window. He saw a huge fireball in the distance as the plane moved closer and closer to the ground.

The skilled pilot was able to guide the plane to an emergency landing, but not without sacrifice. He rested it on a highway not far from the mountain, veering off the pavement to avoid stopped cars. The landing gear failed and the plane bounced as it rolled belly down across the rough terrain

Moments before the plane came to a stop it spun and rolled.

Parker found himself face down near a window. There was a coffee carafe and cups by his head.

His forehead hurt and burned, he brought his fingers to his head feeling wetness. Blood.

"Everyone okay?" he called out.

He heard a cough.

"Charles, that you?"

"I think I broke my ribs," Charles said. "Otherwise I'm fine."

"That was close." Parker stumbled as he stood. "It landed close." He tried to look around for Charles, unable to see him. Then the bright sun burst through when an emergency door opened.

"President Wesley, sir," a soldier called out. "We need to get you off the plane."

Parker was worried about the others, as they escorted him through the wreckage, he looked around and he saw the bodies of those who didn't move, some bleeding, some struggling to get up.

He was worried, how injured were they? Did he really need to be a priority when he was able bodied? Could he help?

But all everyone seemed concerned with was getting him from the plane and quickly into the jeep that arrived within minutes. He was hustled into the vehicle and whisked away without Charles.

He was the president. They needed to get him to safety. All Parker could wonder was, with all that was going on, did it really matter who he was? Being the president and having all the bells and whistles didn't mean anything at that moment. It didn't stop the plane from crashing and it certainly didn't stop the rocks hurling in from space.

SEVENTEEN

PRESENT

Los Angeles, California

When CJ was thirteen years old his parents moved to a rural area outside of the city. His father had landed a principal's position in the local school. Near their home was a large local farm, the fields of which spanned across the two lane, main road.

He remembered going to the store of that farm with his mother and watching the workers being carted across the fields. A pick-up truck towed a large open trailer, similar to ones landscapers used. Only that trailer carried workers, tired and sweaty, transporting them after a long day's work.

He thought of those days as he sat in a trailer just like that, and like the farmworkers he was dirty and exhausted.

At least he got to stop.

He and Mindy had made it about three miles when the truck pulled over and picked them up. There were others in the back, sitting alongside lawnmowers and other equipment.

Mindy hadn't said much since they left Dallas. He figured she was tired and things were catching up to her. She rested her head against his shoulder, fell asleep, still holding her phone.

Crammed and crowded, uncomfortable or not, it was a ride and CJ was grateful for that.

The longer they were in the truck, the smoother the ride. There was less destruction, and cars moved about the debris strewn streets, more people were not at the mercy of trying to find a ride.

When they were offered a ride the driver told them he would get them and the others to the Convention Center. There they could get a ride needed to higher ground. He himself had family and friends he had to get, and he needed the room in the truck.

CJ was fine with that. He hated to leave the area, hated running to the proverbial hills. He knew, though, he couldn't go back.

His best shot of finding his family was to get to civilization and areas untouched by the disaster, because he was confident that his father, if alive, would get Carter out of the danger zone.

Once they arrived and disembarked from the back of the truck, CJ realized that not only finding his father was going to be a task, but getting a ride to higher ground would be like finding the Holy Grail.

The entire area around the Convention Center was crammed packed with people. Shoulder to shoulder, arguing and angry. There were perhaps a dozen vehicles parked and people fought violently to get on one of them. They shoved and fought, screaming at each other, while children cried.

There was no way he and Mindy were going to get on one of the few transports, unless more showed up.

He didn't know when the wave would arrive, but he was sure that it would be there long before everyone was evacuated.

"This doesn't look good," Mindy said.

"No, it doesn't."

"How are we supposed to get out of here?" Mindy asked. "I mean, there are too many people and not enough vehicles."

"We're just going to have to …" CJ's eyes widened. "Wait."

"We can't wait."

"No, I mean, wait … wait." He looked around. "Dallas."

"We're in Los Angeles."

"I know that. I mean … Dallas and his father. They said it was the third truck they had, right?"

Mindy nodded.

"Downtown is largely unscathed. If Dallas and his father can find a truck in the rubble, we can find something around here."

"How?"

"Charlton Heston."

"Who?"

CJ waved out his hand. "Never mind. Just know he was an actor, in a post apocalypse movie that took place right here in LA. When he needed a new car, he just grabbed one from a dealership."

"Wait." Mindy gasped. "There's a whole bunch of them a few blocks away."

"Exactly. There has to be at least enough gas in the tanks for a test drive, which means enough gas to get us to higher ground."

"Can we get the keys?" she asked.

"Probably a lot faster than getting on a bus." He took her hand. "Let's go." They were already at the edge of the hoard of people, and CJ led her quickly away from the lot of the convention center to the street.

He was moving so determined and fast that he stepped toward the street and stopped just before a bus laid on its horn and then slammed on its brakes nearly hitting them.

It was close.

Too close.

Catching his breath and frazzled, CJ reacted by yelling out, 'Hey', slamming his hand into the side of the stopped bus. Just as he stepped back to keep moving, he looked up and froze.

Guy and Carter sat three rows from the front on the gray prison bus that was used to transport them. Because of Carter, and his age, they were first to board in the evacuation to higher ground. Ruben was seated in the row in front of them, next to an elderly woman who had to be at least eighty.

Ruben hadn't said much since the bus arrived, still torn and shaken by Roger's death. He stared forward barely responding to the conversation the woman tried to have with him.

It was perfect seating, though. While Carter slept Guy was able to listen to the radio chatter between the bus driver and whoever it was he communicated with.

'We have about nine spots,' the driver said over the radio shortly after they left.

'Roger that, if you can pick up that would work. We can notify the convention center.'

'I prefer not to. I have a lot of elderly and children on board. I'd like to continue to Elysian."

"That would be a negative. Elysian is scratched. Pick up as many as you can and continue west. Sixty is clear, low traffic, continue that route to San Bernardino. Refuel at the airport and radio back for directives"

"Roger that. Can I ask why?"

"We'll have more details once you are clear of Los Angeles."

San Bernardino? Guy wasn't knowledgeable of the area, but he was certain that was a lot farther than they needed to go to clear the wave. If indeed, that was why they were moving inland.

He supposed he'd find out, either when they got there or by listening to the radio talk. Either way, they were safe.

He had a view through the windshield by leaning into the aisle, and Guy was happy to see that Downtown Los Angeles suffered minimal damage. The quake was nearer to the coast and those in the city were more than likely able to move out on their own if they followed the evacuation order.

He reached up and tapped Ruben on the shoulder. "Everything looks good out here. We'll be able to contact our families soon."

Ruben just nodded.

Guy was pleased. His apocalyptic visions and fears were put to ease when he saw unscathed buildings. To him they had seen the worst of it, been through the worst and soon would get help. The rest of the world had to be alright.

He turned to Carter who stared out the window. "See?" he said to the boy. "Everything is okay. We'll be out of this soon, we can get in touch with your mom and find your father."

As soon as he said that the bus jolted hard and Guy flew forward catching himself before he slammed into the seat in front of him.

"Sorry," the bus driver called out. "Jesus, look at this crowd."

Guy leaned in toward the aisle again to see. People blocked the road, banged on the bus and screamed to get on it.

The bus driver picked up the radio. "This is Evac seventeen. Change of plans. There is no way we can stop. Too many people. I can't risk those on the bus."

"Roger that seventeen, proceed to evacuation route."

Guy sat back and relaxed. He felt the bus inch forward and begin to turn.

"Dad." Carter said softly, then lifted the volume of his voice. "Dad!"

Guy turned quickly in the seat.

Carter faced the window fully, his hands flush against the glass as he screamed out.

Guy looked. CJ stood on the side of the road with Mindy and Guy smiled. His son was alive.

"Stop the bus!" Guy yelled. "Stop the bus. My son is out there."

"I can't do that," the driver replied. "There's too many out there. They'll rush the bus."

"But my son ..."

"I'm sorry."

The bus started to turn.

Guy jumped toward the window. His fingers fiddled with the slide locks excitedly, pushing them outward to lower the window.

He dropped the window as the bus inched away and Guy stuck his head out the window.

CJ saw him. He knew he son saw him.

"He won't stop!" Guy yelled. "San Bernardino airport. We're headed there!"

"Dad!" Carter poked his head out the window next to Guy. "Daddy!"

CJ waved and ran toward the bus. "I'll meet you there. Wait for me. I'll meet you ... there."

The bus pulled further away, and Guy watched his son until he couldn't see him anymore.

He sat down and embraced Carter. "He made it. He made it."

"He saw us, right? He saw us?" Carter asked.

"He saw us. He'll find us," Guy said. "We'll be together soon."

Ruben turned around in his seat. "I'm happy for you."

"Yeah," Guy said. "Me, too."

With a 'whew' and an exhale, Guy relaxed. All his fears had been relieved. The destruction seemed to end and his son was alive and well.

Everything was going to be fine.

Like excited school girls at a concert, CJ and Mindy embraced, jumping up and down, excitedly exclaiming, "They're alive. They're alive."

"Oh, CJ," Mindy gushed. "This is great. "

"I know. If that bus wouldn't have almost hit me, I wouldn't have seen them."

"But they're going to San Bernardino? That's over fifty miles away. That's further than higher ground. Why do you think they're going there?"

"I don't know. I don't care. They're alright. We know where they are. Let's go." With enthusiasm and renewed vigor, holding Mindy's hand he moved, rushing toward the area of town with the slew of car dealerships.

One way or another he would find a vehicle.

He had a destination and his family.

CJ felt good, optimistic. He would be with his father and son soon.

The worst he believed was over with.

Cheyenne Mountain, Colorado

When he arrived at Cheyenne Mountain the day before, injured and confused, Parker saw the effect of the rushed effort to preserve not only what they could of the government, but ensure the survival of those who could help with some sort of law and order when it all fell apart and it was well on its way.

Military trucks carrying soldiers and supplies formed a long convoy on the road to the mountain.

When the last of the trucks had finally arrived, the gates were closed and sealed, despite the reports of the growing number of civilians that had made a pilgrimage to the mountain in hopes of salvation and safety. Civilians who watched their homes crumble.

Now he sat, slightly rested, several sutures in his head, trying to take it all in.

Gary Boothe, an astrophysicist and geologist from NASA, had the floor, complete with images that were projected on the large screen behind him. It was split screen, divided in four. The top two images were taken in space of the asteroids and the bottom images were earth, each marked and color coded. Blue were the areas affected by water and flooding. Red was impact sites, orange were areas affected by seismic activity, and there were purple circles that hadn't been explained.

Parker rubbed his chin hard, the whiskers from his five o'clock shadow were abrasive on his hand. His eyes shifted from the images on the wall to the monitors that showed the people gathering outside.

"The Atlantic wave started in New York," Gary explained, "Making its way down the entire eastern seaboard. It washed in a hundred and twelve miles. Everything on the coast within thirty miles is gone."

"So we lost New York, Washington..." Parker started the list.

Gary nodded. 'Philly, Florida."

"Florida is a state."

"It's under about ten feet of water right now. It will recede … eventually." Gary cleared his throat. "The three meteorites that impacted the Atlantic, landed so close to shore, there wasn't time to issue an evacuation. We are making that attempt now in the west."

Charles leaned into Parker. "We have choppers warning. National Guard has been deployed and right now are trying to move as many people as we can."

"Can we?" Parker asked.

"As many as we can. They have about two hours to get to higher ground. It's not looking good."

"I'm looking at this …" Parker stood and pointed to the map. "Is this the seismic activity that's from the impact sites?"

"More or less," Gary replied. "While these are categorized as meteorites, I'd say they are borderline asteroids. When they hit, the immediate area is flattened, gone. The impact causes a fireball and the blast winds can travel close to five hundred miles, the closer you are, the more damage. Earthquakes of seven, eight, even nine on the Richter scale can travel hundreds of miles around the epicenter. However, this is just the tip of the iceberg. These hits have triggered a chain reaction that is getting out of control."

"Explain chain reaction."

"We aren't just having earthquakes from the impact. Here …" he pointed to the coast of California, then to the Midwest around Kentucky. "Here." And his hand moved north toward the Pennsylvania area. "And here, for example it's genuine seismic activity. The quakes in these regions are expanding outward, they will continue for a while."

"How?" Parker asked. "I mean, I'm confused. The earthquakes are residual from the impact, right?"

"Yes and no," Gary said. "Think about legs. Old legs. Perhaps your grandmother's legs. All veiny and lined."

"Oh, Dear God," Parker said.

"That's the United States."

"I am to liken the US to my grandmother's varicose veins?"

Gary nodded. "Only those veins are fault lines. There are hundreds of fault lines in the US, but there are five major areas. And they are where I just pointed. If Grandma had a big varicose vein in her knee and was hit by a baseball right on that vein or close, that vein could burst, or start bleeding beneath the skin. The blood would spread out, causing pain in a wider area. The vein could even rupture, and there's nothing that can be done until the vein heals … or ruptures then the after effects kill her."

Charles raised his hand slightly. "So the fault lines, like say, Andreas or Cascadia are Grandma's veins and the meteor is the baseball they were hit with."

"A line drive."

Parker shook his head. "I liked the darts and globes analogy better."

"The veins were a good analogy." Charles sat back. "So they are all active now?"

"Every one of them," Gary answered. "And there is nothing we can do but wait it out. Then … then we can see where we stand and what you need to do to initiate the best chance of long term survival for as many as you can."

"How long?" Parker asked. "Days, weeks?"

Gary shrugged. "I'd be guessing. Major quakes, the next couple of days, each of them diminishing in intensity."

"Right now we're in the second wave of meteorites," Parker said. "Once they hit, and there isn't that many, we can start to assess."

"Um ... No." Gary shook his head. "The meteorites are problem number one, massive Fault line activity… problem two."

"Why do I have a feeling I'm not going to like problem three?"

Gary pointed to the map. "See these areas of purple?" he indicted to the various shades in circles, ranging from deep to light.

"I was wondering wwhat they were," Parker said.

"These two dark spots represent Long Valley Caldera and

Yellowstone. I haven't even touched Mount St. Helens or Rainer."

Parker blinked long. "They're all going to blow."

"They are. I mean we could be wrong, but I doubt it. I'm saying days at most, maybe even hours. With this much seismic activity, they're already letting off steam."

Parker sighed out. "The ruptured vein." He walked closer to the map. "California is purple, the entire area is purple. What about those being evacuated? They're going to higher ground, but they aren't out of danger, are they?"

Gary shook his head. 'No. Not for a while. They'll have to keep going east. Southeast at first then make their way north, somewhere after Texas. They can survive the eruption in California, but the after-effects of the volcano will decrease survivability. And realistically, you aren't going to be able to move all those people. If the eruption does happen, the ash alone will inhibit any travel. It'll choke out all engines."

"This isn't good."

"No, it's bad."

Charles asked. "Is there anything we can do in the meantime?"

"If the Midwest region of Ohio, Michigan and parts of Canada make it through this next series of impacts, you can focus there."

"What about us?" Parker asked. "We're close to Yellowstone."

"We are," Gary replied. "Fortunately, we are not in the kill zone. Unfortunately, between Long Valley and Yellowstone, like a bad case of food poisoning, we're gonna get hit at both ends."

Parker cringed. "Can you stop with the analogies?" he turned and when he did he looked at the monitor showing the people gathering outside. "What about them? What happens with them when the eruption occurs?"

"They'll have to move on or they'll die."

"How many are out there?" he asked Charles.

"Several hundred," Charles answered. "Why?"

"Let them in," Parker said.

"Excuse me? We are already going to be strained on supplies as it is."

"Then we'll strain more. Send our units out to salvage as much as they can from anywhere they can. But I will not have those people die out there. They're hurt, scared and need help. Open the gate," Parker said. "Let them in."

EIGHTEEN

Los Angeles, California

Her name was Stacy, but her name no longer was important. The young mother would be one of millions whose hopes, dreams, life and body would be washed away in a second.

When the first quake hit, she raced from her apartment, nine month old baby daughter in one arm and a toddler son on her hip. She made it out safe and sound, fleeing from flying debris. Still clad in pajamas, raced out into the street, dodging items which rained down on her from above.

She didn't know where to run or what to do.

The ground shook while she was making lunch. At first she did what she was supposed to do, stood under a sturdy doorframe. But the more the floor shook, the more Stacy thought, 'this isn't going to work'. Once outside, Stacy viewed her safety options amidst the shaking ground.

The parking lot was her best choice and she fought to keep her balance, as she hustled, barefoot to an empty area of the parking.

When the second big quake came, she watched everything just fall down around her. Then shortly after things settled, the biggest of them all arrived, ensuring that nothing was standing in her area.

She was scared. Her husband had not returned home from the night shift at the airport. She feared he'd never get home. Her first priority, and what he would want, was to take care of the kids.

Neighbors huddled together, making tents. Gathering blankets from cars and rubble. Using them and drapery to create tents over spaced between remaining cars. Placing the fabric in the car door to hold it up.

They lit fires, stayed warm, shared food and helped each other with any medical needs. Those still standing searched though the ruins for survivors who could still be alive.

Then the final and fateful one hit.

Stacy believed she had been blessed. Angels watched over her making sure she was in the right place at the right time.

Everything erupted around her.

Just before the ground lifted a wave of pressure and wind blasted by her and she was shielded. The car in front of her lifted and flipped over the heads of her and the children.

After that, the sky was roaring red in the distance, there was nothing left around them and she and the others began walking to the pilgrimage east.

That was two in the morning.

They walked all night until morning, listening to the overhead announcements to evacuate and get to higher ground.

At an excruciating slow pace they made their way toward downtown Los Angles. Twelve miles. Strangers helped her carry the baby when her back ached and a woman found her shoes to wear just at the point Stacy's feet started to bleed.

She trudged on, it was the only way.

Three miles from downtown, a military tuck stopped to pick up her, the kids and two others from their walking group. Those who looked vulnerable and weak.

It felt good to stop, to rest, even if it was only a few minutes.

Stacy was proud of her children. With all they had been through, they were remarkably quiet and rarely cried.

They had survived everything thrown at them, there was no reason to believe they wouldn't survive the impending wave.

Stacy began to doubt that the second they arrived in Los Angeles.

There were more people than she expected, all crammed together around the convention center, waiting to get a seat on one of the few buses there.

More vehicles arrived, people with regular trucks, offering to take a few. Had Stacy not gotten out of that truck, she probably would have gotten a ride. A part of her believed there would be a seat for everyone. She had no idea the vehicle was pushing forward. She thought it was going back for more people.

But as the vehicles moved out, the crowd grew agitated, and it became hostile.

They fought and banged on buses and any means of transportation that passed them by. The hordes of desperate people pushed and shoved forcing Stacy to back up for the safety of her kids.

That only pushed her further behind.

Cars came from nowhere with no regard to how they drove. They plowed through the crowds, hitting innocent bystanders even as they kept on going.

People fought for a seat on the bus or a place to stand in the aisle.

Finally, Stacy was close. She was three people from getting on the bus and suddenly they stopped taking more.

"We're full. We don't even have room to stand."

"Please," Stacy begged. "Please take my children. Please."

The driver got on the bus and closed the doors.

Stacy shouted and pleaded to those who stared out the window. Begging for someone to reach out and take her baby.

No one did.

Then the last of the busses and trucks rolled out. Stacy stood there. Her baby in her arms as she held her son close to her hip.

When fifteen or so minutes went by and no more vehicles arrived Stacy knew her chance to catch a ride was over.

Hundreds of people were stranded.

The intensity level increased when people started shouting that the wave was coming. How they knew, Stacy hadn't a clue.

It all went absolutely insane.

Within minutes of that rumor, dozens of helicopters flew overhead, all going east as emergency sirens blasted in the air.

As if things weren't chaotic enough, that send people into a tailspin,

They all began to run.

When the crowd around her thinned out and dispersed, that was when she heard it.

The faint roar of water in the distance.

"Oh my God."

Higher ground. Higher ground.

She looked around.

A building.

It was a block down the street and had to be ten stories high. That had to be high enough. They were a good distance from the shore, how high could that wave possibly be?

Others ran toward that building, as it was the closest, and Stacy joined them.

It was amazing to her how much fear, worry and adrenaline fueled the body when it needed it.

Clutching both her children, she raced to the building, following others inside. It was dark and without power. She trailed behind those who ran to the stairwell.

She wasn't fast.

Physically there was no way she was anywhere near as fast as others. They ran by her. Shoving into her, but Stacy kept going.

Heart pounding in her chest, so much she felt it in her ears, her breath was literally gone as she made it to the top and saw the light of day as it peeked through the door to the roof.

She did it. She had made it. She was there and safe.

With the last bit of her energy, her toddler son dangling in her embrace, Stacy burst through the open door.

It was loud.

Not the dozens of people on the roof, but the ocean. She could hear how threatening it sounded.

Where? Where was it?

Finally she saw the direction everyone faced.

She joined the group, looking outward. At first it was hard to see, the color blended into the skyline, then she saw it moving. It moved with a vengeance, full of debris, sweeping up and gathering everything in its path.

"We'll be okay," someone said. "It doesn't look that high."

"It's not high," another said with enthusiasm. "We made it."

But it was only their perception, not reality.

The wave *was* that high and the closer it drew the more Stacy saw the destruction it caused, crashing through overpasses causing them to crumble. It wasn't the water as much as it was the cars and debris it brought with it.

Stacy had one choice.

She couldn't run or hide.

All that she had gone through wasn't building to her survival, it was building to her end. It wasn't fair, but what could she do.

She clutched her children tightly, told them how much she loved them, and whispered a prayer that they wouldn't be frightened or feel any pain.

Her eyes stayed focused on the water and only closed them when it arrived.

There was an eruption of screams and then it slammed through.

The moment it collided with her, Stacy was lifted and moved backward. Her legs kicked and she struggled against the watery aggressor. It hit her so hard, her skin burned with the sting and pain as the bones in her body break. The pain of the impact was excruciating, but not as much as the heartache when she realized her hands were empty.

She had lost her children, they were ripped from her arms with the fury of the raging ocean.

Once she knew they were gone she closed her eyes again, extended out her arms, allowing the water to move her, she accepted her fate.

NINETEEN

Cheyenne Mountain, Colorado

Wearing jeans, a t-shirt and baseball cap was like a disguise for Parker. No one seemed to recognize him as he moved about the refugees that were setting up camp in the hallways until everything was organized. He worked alongside the workers, trying to register everyone and seeing what they needed. Passing out, food, water and blankets.

Charles looked irritated, standing in the hall, waving to get Parker's attention. He had moved around the people there, it was like walking through a maze. Parker knew him well enough to know that at some point Charles gave up on making it through the people and opted for waving.

Parker made his way to Charles.

"What's going on?"

"Do you have some time for an update?"

"Absolutely."

Placing his hand on Parker's back, he guided him down the hall to a more private area and into a small office.

In the office was a table, and it reminded Parker of the interrogation rooms of television police shows. He sat at the table when Charles shut the door.

"I know how you dislike the long technical versions," Charles said. "I'll give you what I have and let you get back to your Florence Nightingallery."

"Interesting term."

"Made it up myself. Alright ..." Charles dropped a folder on the table, sat, and then opened the folder. "We brought in six hundred and forty-three people, four dogs, two cats, two horses, a chicken and a cow."

"A cow?"

"A cow."

"Wow."

"Yeah. Anyhow … we are crunching numbers and assessing what we can do. We hope to have everyone given some sort of living arrangements by tomorrow night."

"That's good."

"There are certain areas we cannot have civilians, we need that as work space. We sent out the trucks to salvage what they could from local warehouses. We have equipment here to care for four hundred people for one year. Bear in mind, two thirds of those four hundred are military personnel, many of which will be part of survivor sweeps when the proverbial dust settles."

"So, we're one and a half times what we have supplies for?" Parker asked.

"We're hopeful our salvaging will bring more. Without it, we're looking at four months tops with supplies. That is not going to be ideal. We won't have a long term survival plan finished by then."

"We should have a working idea, though, right?"

Charles nodded. "We're working on it now. But there is nothing we can do until we make it through the global catastrophes. Until we can see what is still standing, what is the least unscathed, it's all guess work."

"We have people on this. Experts. What are they saying? How long until we know something?"

"Could be weeks."

"Weeks?" Parker exclaimed in shock. "I thought it was forty-eight hours of impacts."

"That's without volcanic activity and further waves. Realistically, Yellowstone isn't going to go boom and that's it. She'll more than likely continuously erupt for weeks. Less if we're lucky."

"We don't know if it is going to erupt for sure," Parker said. "I mean, people have been saying that for decades."

"Um … yes, but this series of natural disasters and events is unprecedented in any recorded history. As Gary told us, it's a chain of events we're not going to be able to stop. We have to wait."

"Gary?" Parker asked.

"The geologist, astrophysicist NASA guy we brought."

"Him. Yes. King of analogies. And Yellowstone is one of those events?"

"Along with other volcanoes and calderas. Yellowstone is not the only one. Long Valley Caldera in California is nearly as big and is close to the Nevada border. We know that Long Valley is going to erupt and it is imminent. We may not have satellite contact, but we have eyes on the ground there."

"How?"

"A man named Lowell on Mammoth Mountain, which is right near the Long Valley Caldera. We made radio contact. He said the ground has continuously been shaking, steam and ash have been pouring into the sky and the ground is swelling."

"Why is he there? Should he be evacuated?"

"He won't go. He is handicapped. In a wheel chair and he said, and I quote, 'I'm old. I have lived here my entire life and if this thing is gonna blow, then damn it I am watching it'. He said he will keep us updated until … well, he can't."

Parker whistled. "God bless him. What about our evacuees on the West Coast?"

"We evacuated sixty percent of those who needed transportation."

"Sixty percent? That's it."

"It's better than the overall predictions. We did the best we could. We haven't received any word on how much damage, or how far the devastation from wave went. We're still trying to establish links to our satellites. But we had sixty percent of the people moved. To where, we don't know. We're going to keep going and refuel until we can't."

"Is that an overall prediction?"

Charles nodded. "If this plays out the way it is predicted. The triggered faults, volcanic eruptions and tsunamis from the eruptions, along with the debris up in the air is going to cause rain and flooding. We won't even talk about what is going to come down with the rain. Add that to the already devastated areas from the impacts … we're talking a seventy-percent loss of life in the US."

"Oh my God." Parker ran his hand down his face. "How can you say that so calmly and matter of fact?"

"Hysterics won't change a thing."

"So in a nutshell, Mother Nature is cleaning house."

"Unfortunately," Charles said with a nod. "And she's not playing around."

San Bernardino Airport

Guy remembered when CJ was nine and he took him to an air show. He thought about that day with his son because the San Bernardino Airport reminded him of that show on a larger scale.

Airplanes took off one after another with very few time in between. Down the runway, into the air, then the next would line up. It was a continuous flow of planes.

The buses, tractor trailers and other vehicles were lined up for the pumps and fueling trucks. It was advised that no one leave the buses or their vehicles, once fueled they rolled out.

The city had been ordered to evacuate.

Guy didn't understand why. They weren't near the water or the wave. From the looks of things the town suffered minimal damage from quakes.

Then again, Guy hadn't heard the news or a radio.

No one really knew anything. Just that they had to keep moving.

Guy couldn't or rather, he wouldn't.

It was a source of great debate for him. He had Carter to protect and he had a son of his own out there.

After hearing rumors that the east has suffered devastation, Guy was left to wonder … where exactly was he going? Where were they all going and why? Guy hadn't processed it. He was too focused on saving Carter and staying alive. They lived right outside of D.C., and if Joel, the radio guy was correct, D.C. was gone. At least it was what Joel was able to piece together.

It seemed ridiculous to head home, when home was probably gone. Aside from that, there was no home without CJ. So Guy took Carter by the hand, left the bus and walked across the large airfield under the menacing overcast skies to the terminal.

He told his son he would meet him at the airport. There wasn't any reason to believe CJ wasn't showing up. He just hadn't yet.

When Guy arrived at the terminal it was empty and scary. Like something out of a Stephen King novel. Not a soul in the airport, papers scattered about on the floor, luggage and carryon's had just been abandoned. There was a security cart parked inside the front doors. No driver, just the flashing light.

There were no airport sounds, no music, nothing.

Guy stood inside the open sliding glass doorways of the departure terminal, there was no power and the door was stuck open. He stood not far from the ticket counter, staring out. When CJ arrived he would come that way, so he would see him.

Carter was finally energized, and his resiliency seemed to chuck his near-death experience to the curb, as he explored the area behind Guy.

"Not too far. Stay where I can hear you," Guy told him.

"Can we look around?"

"Once your father gets here," Guy said. "Then we'll figure out the next step."

When Guy left the bus, they were four or five from the end of the line. He supposed they were all gone by now.

Focused on watching the road, Guy perked up when he saw a car approach. He smiled, watching the car pull into the garage across the road, parking inside, under cover.

"What the heck?" Guy asked out loud. "Now why would he park?"

"Is my dad here?" Carter ran toward him.

Just as he was about to tell him that CJ had arrived, he saw the man step from the car.

Ruben.

Guy stepped outside. "Ruben?" he hollered. "What are you doing? Why aren't you on the bus?"

Ruben carried a back pack and jotted his way to Guy. "I got us a car. Just in case. I figured it would be safe under there."

"What are you doing? Why are you here?"

"You didn't even wait for me."

"I told you I was staying and waiting on CJ."

"And you really expected me to keep going on the bus? Guy, come on," Ruben said. "They don't even know where they're going."

"Neither do we."

"At least I know you, right? Hey, we started this journey together, we'll finish it together."

"Thank you." Guy shook his hand. "I appreciate it."

Ruben stepped inside. "Wow, this is weird. It's empty. The whole city is a ghost town."

"It's also scary," Guy said. "We don't know why the area was evacuated."

"I spoke to a man who helped me with the car. He told me he was from the area and it was just a precaution, the area was fragile and prone to further quakes."

"Swell."

"Some are headed to the mountains," Ruben said. "Most are just headed east."

Guy stepped closer to Ruben and whispered. "But you heard what Joel said."

"I did. East is bad, West is bad. Maybe somewhere in the middle is fine."

Guy looked over his shoulder to check on Carter. "At least he's oblivious."

"That's a good thing and so is this place." Ruben looked around. "It's not damaged at all. We have shelter. We may be fine. I haven't felt a tremor in a while."

"I don't trust anything anymore. Everything keeps going to hell in a handbag on a dime." Guy walked nearer the door and sighed out heavily. "We left hours ago to head sixty miles. Hours. We saw CJ when we were leaving. Where is he?"

"Guy, we sat in traffic for an hour. We're part of an exodus. He's behind us. He probably had to find a vehicle. Maybe he even searched for another way. He's with Mindy. She's knows the area. He'll be here." Ruben gave a pat to Guy's back. "I'm positive. He's fine."

Guy only nodded. He appreciated Ruben's optimism, but he himself had a hard time feeling it. And he supposed he wouldn't feel better until he saw his son.

Where was he?

CJ wasn't the only one who had the bright idea to take a car from a dealership. Mindy felt bad for him. His already bruised body took a beating as he fought for the access to keys. She lost a section of her hair when some woman grabbed her. She could feel the hair rip from the roots. She ended up grabbing a chair and acting like a lion tamer in some sort of protective stance from the masses.

Keys were grabbed and she saw the one drop to the floor and slide across. No one else saw it and Mindy hurriedly stepped on it.

When the last of the keys were gone, and a riot broke out, smashing windows that weren't destroyed in the quake. Mindy let CJ know she had keys. She didn't want to tip her hand before that.

They ended up with a set with no identification tag. Only a lock and unlock remote that CJ kept pressing, hoping that he'd get close enough to hear a 'blip-blip'.

Finally, they heard the sound and rushed toward it, finding a ten year old four door sedan.

They hurriedly got inside and took off. They didn't make it far, when they saw an elderly couple, frantically waving for them to stop.

CJ passed them, then decency hit him. He stopped, backed up and allowed for Rose and Marty to get inside. A few seconds later, people rushed them and they couldn't take the chance of stopping again.

There was traffic, but not as much as would have been expected from an area with ten million people.

That was when it hit Mindy how many people were killed.

She didn't want to say anything, but she had seen less traffic than at rush hour.

Even with minimal traffic, it seemed they weren't making any progress, that was when she suggested another route. They veered off the main road just as sirens began to blare.

"Keep East. Keep east. Don't stop," she urged.

"You said the waves move about twenty miles an hour, right?" CJ asked.

"Once they make landfall, yes," Mindy answered, then looked behind her.

"Anything there?" CJ asked.

"No. We can stay ahead of it. I'll tell you where to go. Keep driving."

CJ followed her directions. Mindy was fearful that any hold up, any detour would cause them to succumb to the wave.

But they stayed ahead of it, as far as they could see, even making it to a secondary main road that seemed like clear sailing. Once he saw a sign that indicated San Bernardino was thirty-two miles, Mindy felt relieved. They beat it.

They were home free.

Rose and Marty were a couple in their late seventies. Thankful for the ride and upset. They lived in an apartment downtown. Marty was a retired architect and talked about how the buildings would withstand the pressure of the water.

"We just don't know how high the wave is," he said. "If we could have stayed ahead of it and gotten to a top floor, we would have made it. I'm sure. Problem was, there's no power. Rose and I couldn't make it up that far."

"Thank you," Rose reached up and patted CJ on the shoulder. "Thank you."

"Don't thank me yet," CJ replied. "We don't know where we're going after."

"After?" Rose asked.

"My father and son were on a bus headed to San Bernardino airport. He is meeting us there. I don't know where we'll go after."

"East," Rose said. "They said on the radio to go east."

Mindy turned around in her seat. "You had a radio?"

"Up until this morning. It was emergency broadcasting. Then we lost power."

Mindy made eye contact with CJ, then she reached for the radio. It didn't even dawn on her to turn it on. She did.

A robotic sounding voice was in the middle of stating areas that were under mandatory evacuation and for people to go east. No direction, no location or indication how far they were to travel. It didn't say 'why', the only specific information given was the counties under a tsunami warning.

That, to her made sense, but when they started mentioning counties farther east, Mindy suspected something else was up.

Another meteor perhaps?

"Rose, was this what you heard?" Mindy asked. "Or did you hear something else?" she turned her head to look at the couple in the back seat.

The couple cuddled together, like two teenagers. Mindy smiled a little and then she saw something. She tilted her head and squinted her eyes.

The traffic behind them was moving weird, it looked like three lanes on a two lane road. And if she wasn't mistaken, she swore she saw a shopping cart rolling down the highway.

Then she realized what was causing the strange optical illusion.

"Oh my God, CJ, floor it."

"What?" CJ asked.

"Floor it."

CJ looked to the rear view mirror and slammed the gas hard. The engine revved and the car jolted forward.

Despite how hard she tried to see the water, she couldn't. But Mindy knew it was there and was the culprit.

"It's not deep," Marty said. "We must be close to where it will finish. It has to break soon."

"Drive," urged Rose.

Mindy turned in her seat and watched as it moved closer.

It wasn't the height of the water that was threatening, it was everything that water brought with it. Cars, pieces of buildings, roofs, all rolled their way. Like an avalanche gathering strength as it moved forward. The scariest was the tractor trailer … coming closer … closer.

"How's it look? CJ asked.

"Drive. Just drive," said Mindy. "Faster."

She could see the headlights, then as the truck slanted sideways she saw the panicked driver inside.

"It won't go faster!" CJ yelled.

Mindy realized at that moment, as the car swerved slightly, they were hydroplaning. CJ grabbed the wheel to control the vehicle.

The water flowed under the truck first … then SLAM.

There was not only no escaping the water, there was no escaping the truck.

The force of the eighteen wheeler lifted the car then flipped it front end forward and it crashed down on something.

Mindy didn't know what.

The impact set off a sequence of 'pops' and the airbags inflated. One smacked her in the face and the side panel shoved her sideways.

The rolling car was out of control, but they heard continuous bangs. It truck ricocheted off whatever was in the water, they saw nothing but a series of flashing visions. Bits and pieces of CJ jolting, his hands lifting from the wheel and items which flew around the car. At some point a window broke and the glass floated around the car in what looked like slow motion.

Finally, the car stopped rolling and spinning, glided a few feet upside down than came to an abrupt halt.

Mindy had only a moment to shake off the confusion, then water started poured in. She took a deep breath and braced herself.

Her hands shook and struggled with the usually easy task of undoing the seat belt, as her head submerged instantly. She braced herself to drop when she finally released the seat belt. She slipped downward and as she maneuvered her legs she saw CJ, he was submerged and struggling, and in the back seat, Marty kicked against the back door while holding a motionless Rose.

Thinking fast, Mindy assisted CJ, once his belt released she swam out of the broken windshield. It didn't take much to get out of the car and it took only for her to stand and she emerged from the water.

Their upside-down car was one of many in a sea of water no deeper than four feet.

Making her way around to the side of the car, she heaved in a deep breath, went under and pulled on the rear passenger door.

It opened only a third of the way, but enough for Marty to push out Rose.

Mindy took hold of the petite woman, guiding her up and out of the water.

Using her body, she braced the woman against the car to keep her head upward.

"Rose," she called her. "Rose. Rose."

Rose's head bled a little near the eye.

Mindy shook her, pushing against her stomach with her own body because it was the only option she had to try to get any water out of her.

From the corner of her eye, she spotted Marty as he stood. "Rose!" he called out.

It was as if his voice was what Rose needed to hear, a split second after he yelled for her, she choked, coughed and spat water.

"I got her," Marty said. "I got her."

Once Mindy was certain he did, she moved from his way and looked around. She breathed heavily, trying to slow her heart rate as she scanned around for CJ.

She spotted him in the distance, sludging through the water, aimlessly and confused.

"CJ!" she yelled to him.

He stopped walking and turned around. Mindy could see the expression on his face. He was relieved and smiled, then rushed her way.

"Are you okay?" he asked when he saw her. "Hurt?"

"I don't think so. I'm cold. You?"

"Shivering, and I'll be happy if I never see the ocean again."

"Yeah, twice in a couple days is too much for me, too."

CJ faced Marty. "You guys alright?"

"Yeah, yeah," Marty nodded. "Rose is weak. We need to get her out of the water."

"Then let's try," CJ said.

Try? How was that even possible, Mindy thought? They'd have to carry her, blindly trudging through the flooded area, with dangers they couldn't see under their feet. They'd have to figure out which way was west. Not easy with the darkening clouded sky. As hard as it sounded, they had no choice. It seemed impossible. It wasn't like the first time they found themselves in water. *This* water didn't funnel its way into a narrower path. There was no dry land to aim for, just three or four feet of water filled with cars and debris. It encircled them, it was everywhere, and seemingly no end in sight.

TWENTY

Cheyenne Mountain

In science fiction movies and books, there always seemed to be a never failing system. Satellite images were conveniently on hand. The president or his staff, if they survived, knew everything. They were on top of the information food chain.

It wasn't that way in reality.

All Parker had was a miracle radio transmission from a man named Lowell, claiming he could see the Caldera ready to blow from his back deck. That was it, of all the destruction, that was the only true information he had other than what he had witnessed first-hand. Which really wasn't much compared to everyone else.

Lowell was a loner, the last remaining person on Mammoth Mountain. Parker had ordered someone to talk to him constantly, keeping the man company.

By the sound of his voice, parker envisioned a man in his sixties, rough and tumbling that had an accident perhaps that left him in a wheelchair.

Probably a two pack a day smoker with a bottle of whiskey never far from his reach. Whether that was true or not, Parker didn't know.

It helped with the visual as he listened to the man's voice coming through the speaker.

"What about us trying to get you out of there," Parker said.

"Nah, that's a negative," Lowell replied. "I'm not going anywhere. Besides, the ash is pretty steady, the rumbling is continuous. Nothing I can't deal with it. She'll blow soon, I feel it, and I can even smell it."

"I'm sorry you're alone."

"Hey, I'm not. I'm talking to the president. I'm gonna leave this earth a pretty important and remembered guy."

"Yes, you will. And we will be here until … until …"

"Transmission stops?" Lowell asked.

"Yes," Parker said. "Yes. Until it stops."

He was getting ready to ask Lowell a little about himself, maybe get him to share a story, when he noticed Charles signaling him.

"Hey, buddy," Parker said. "Have to step out. I'll be back."

"I'm not going anywhere."

Parker pursed his lips. It was a sad thing to know that he was talking to a man who was facing his end.

He stood from the chair and followed Charles to the other side of the communications room. A soldier took the seat where Parker had been and conversed with Lowell.

"What's going on?" Parker asked.

"I have some really good news."

"Everything is done? No more disasters?"

"Not that good."

"What is it?"

"The Russians are still up and running. They said they have been trying to reach out to everyone since the impacts began."

"This is great news. They kept some of their military communications …"

"All."

"Excuse me?"

"Ever play darts with someone really drunk? They hit everything but the dartboard," Charles said. "Russia is the dart board."

"What is it with these damn analogies?" Parker snapped. "And that's impossible."

"Yeah, it is. They are not hit. They didn't sustain any impact. Their science community is putting together reports for us. Rather, everyone they can reach. They reconnected to one of the satellites and are trying to get images."

Parker stared.

"What's wrong? This is great news. We're going to know

what's going on. Right now we are in the dark."

"I know. I know. It's great news. But Russia was completely spared?"

"Completely. God willing, they may not be the only ones," Charles said.

"Hopefully, we'll know soon." Parker nodded. "Thank you. I'm going to go back and talk to Lowell."

"Are you going to share the good news?"

"You mean tell a man who believes he self sacrificed, stayed behind to be the eyes of the world one last time. Tell him that he didn't need to stay back, Russia has it covered?" Parker shook his head. "No. I don't think so."

When Lowell was sixteen years old, he saw an old television show about a crappy motel and a vibrating bed. He never knew those things existed and thought they were a product of a writer's imagination. But the ground beneath him moved at such a steady pace, he thought back to that television show.

He was nauseous. Aside from the constant vibration, the ground rippled in waves as if he were on some sort of amusement park ride.

He felt it overwhelmingly because Lowell was on the ground in the backyard, not far from where his deck collapsed.

His deck was only a couple feet from the ground, more of a wooden patio, so when he and the radio tumbled out, neither of them sustained much damage.

He didn't know how the radio still worked, but it did.

He lost his wheelchair, and without the ability to walk, Lowell lay on the ground, arm aiding to prop him up on his side, watching the sky as it filled with dark gray smoke and ash. He had been on the ground for hours.

The fine granules of the pre eruption state covered him and the ground. He tried hard to keep from breathing it in, but it was difficult. He coughed and choked.

"Yeah," he said into the radio. "I'm still here. I'm not going anywhere." he released the button in the radio.

"Are you scared? Are you worried?" the voice on the other end asked. "I wish here was something we could do."

The last thing Lowell wanted was for someone to think of him as pathetic and weak, so he didn't tell them on the radio that he was laying in the grass with not so much as a glass of water to wet his lips or to coat his dry throat.

"Hey, Lowell, I'm back," the voice switched to that of the president. "How are you doing?"

"I'm fine. Just sipping on a beer, watching the sky."

"It has to be a sight."

"It is. Can I ask you something?" Lowell questioned.

"Yes, you can."

"What happens now? I mean, after the ground stops shaking, heaven quits throwing stuff from the sky, after everything blows and the dust settles. What happens?"

"We're working on that."

"Considering I won't be around. Can you let me know what the plan is?"

"We don't have a concrete plan," Parker said. "We don't know anything. We're trying to get Intel now."

"A lot of people are dead."

"A lot of people are dead," Parker repeated. "The goal is to take those who remain and somehow, get them to an area, where it will be habitable. We're trying to contact areas of FEMA. They have surplus. We get them to move it to those areas. Hopefully soon we'll know what areas they are. Hopefully we can get those supplies."

"It's good to know you have a plan. Keep in mind something Mr. President, the human race is a faulted but resilient species. I believe, when this thing is done, we will rise from the ashes."

Upon his word, finger still depressing the microphone button while he thought of something else to say, Lowell had another thought. He knew instantly, he would not be one of those people who rise from the ashes.

Than it happened. It erupted, even at a distance from him, the sound of the explosion was not something he was ready for or expecting to hear. It sounded so loud, it caused a painful ring in his ear that wasn't going to go away.

His last few seconds would be spent without hearing the roar of devastation he knew the eruption made.

The eruption was three sequential booms that shot earth and fire upward high in the sky. Moments later, that fire transformed into a swirling black cloud that took over the entire horizon. Inside it tiny bits of debris flew about, mixed with flames and sparks.

Lowell tried his best to sit up a little more, not wanting to face his death laying down.

The pyroclastic cloud raced with lightning speed.

He watched it until the wind and heat from it, instinctively caused him to close his eyes.

In seconds, it was over.

There was silence in the control room, complete and utter, stunned silence.

They heard something that sounded like a blip of an explosion, then a rush of static and finally nothing.

Parker lowered his head, then tried one more time. "Lowell. Lowell come in. Lowell."

Nothing.

Parker knew. Everyone knew without saying it ... he was gone.

Lowell's final words were about mankind rising from the ashes. Parker was going to do everything in his power to make sure those last words came true.

TWENTY-ONE

It was worse than trying to make it back to shore. Days as a kid at the beach, when CJ would wander too far out in the ocean. Getting that wave from his father, yelling, "Come back in. Watch out for the rip!"

The water wasn't deep enough to swim, so CJ would do the ocean walk. A marching walk, legs lifting and battling the heavy water as a current hit against the back of his knees, slightly knocking him from his balance.

Only this time there were no soft squishy surfaces, with only sand and seaweed, with the occasional creature to avoid; this time the terrain was rough.

CJ tried to move through the water that came just above his knee.

He felt like he was losing footing every once in a while as he stumbled over cars, pieces of buildings, concrete and bodies that had yet to rise to the surface. That combined with the fact the water felt as if it were moving, pulsing, like waves, making it hard to go forward.

How was that even possible?

It wasn't an easy journey at all. He supposed the water was a bit deeper. He couldn't recall the last time his feet actually touched the ground instead of rubble. Fortunately, CJ and the others were not the only ones to rise from the water and survive the wave. As they moved, others stood as they saw them moving about. Which was a good thing. Because they had Rose. Rose was unable to walk and CJ, along with the kindness of strangers, carried her. They took turns. Handling the fragile woman who toggled between consciousness and sleep.

They were headed in the right direction. They saw a sign, seven more miles to go. It felt like it was a hundred.

Someone asked CJ, "Where are we headed?"

"I don't know where you are headed, but I'm planning on finding my father. He's at the airport."

It seemed as if they just followed him, like he was Moses. Perhaps because he was focused and determined.

Mindy didn't look well. Her face was pale, had he only known her as a popstar he would've figured it was just her stamina giving away. But she had a rough life as a child. The walking and struggling, she knew well. He hoped she wasn't sick or injured.

"I'll take her now." A stranger approached and extended his arms to take Rose from CJ.

"Thank you," CJ replied.

He handed her over gently, and Rose muttered out a soft, "Thank you so much." Before she closed her eyes and rested her head against the stranger.

"Okay," Mindy stepped toward CJ. "You all right? You look kind of pale."

"Me?" CJ chuckled in a tired wave. "You're not looking so hot yourself."

"No, I'm fine. My belly is sore. I bumped it and probably bruised muscle when I was trying to squeeze out that window or something."

"Are you sure?"

"Yep. I'm fine. Now, what about you?"

"I could sure use some of that ibuprofen. I know I will be sore in a little bit."

"We are averaging about a mile an hour." Mindy looked up to the sky. "We will be there by nightfall, maybe shortly after. I'm positive we will find ibuprofen there."

"I'm positive you'll find everything there."

"I plan on it," Mindy said.

CJ lowered his voice. "Do you think … do you think Rose will make it?"

"I think, and …," Mindy said and looked back at the stranger holding Rose and then at Marty. Marty went from person to person, whoever carried his wife he was nearby, wiping her head whispering words of encouragement and love. "I think," Mindy continued. "That question doesn't need to be answered because it doesn't matter. One way or another, we need to make sure that Rose and Marty both get to the airport."

The ticket counter area of the terminal offered cushion bench seats. The ones where travelers sat to put their shoes back on after TSA.

The airport was a plethora of supplies, from food to blankets, even clothes from belongings just left behind. Ruben made his way to a luxury terminal in the next building, he was able to find a little bit more food than what they had on the snack cart.

He grabbed blankets because the temperature was dropping. And before they spoiled, Ruben grabbed some of the deli sandwiches that were in the display cooler of the Grab and Go kiosk.

When he returned back to the main entrance from his brief but productive search, he spotted the orange glow of the campfire Guy had built in the driveway area before the doors.

It was nighttime, and the fire gave light to the ticket counter area.

"Have a sandwich," Ruben extended one to Guy.

"Thank you." Guy took it.

"Nice fire."

"Thank you. Where's Carter? Didn't he go with you?"

"No. he was ..." Ruben turned around. "He was there. Where did he go?'

"He couldn't have gone far." Guy stepped inside the terminal. "Carter!" he hollered. "Carter!'

"Here, Pap." At first his voice was distant, then after the pitter patter of feet, he appeared out of the darkness, as if out of nowhere then into the light. "Here."

"Stay where I can see you."

"Okay." He opened a candy bar.

"Where did you get that?" Guy asked. "You didn't go to the gates did you?'

"No." Carter shook his head. "Her." He pointed backwards.

"Her?" Ruben asked.

Like Carter, a woman stepped from the shadows. Her face was dirty, which hid her age. She was at least forty, her voice had a maturity to it when she spoke. "I didn't think you'd mind if he had candy," she said.

"Who are you?" Guy asked.

"Abby." She extended her hand.

"How long have you been here?" Ruben questioned.

"How long have *you* been here?" she replied, "That's about how long I have been here."

Between chomps of his chocolate bar, Carter said. "She was on the bus with us. I remember."

"You were on the bus?" Guy asked. "Why did you get off?'

"Because you did," she replied.

"Do we know you?" Guy asked.

She shook her head. "No. See when you rushed off the bus with Carter, then he …" She pointed to Ruben. "Rushed off, I was thinking you had some weird Final Destination moment where you saw something horrible happening. Not like things have been a bed of roses. I just couldn't handle any more."

"Why didn't you show yourself earlier?" Guy questioned. "You didn't need to hide."

"I felt bad when I realized the reason you got off was to wait for your son. I mean, I didn't think you were going to live here, I just figured at the very least you had another idea on where to go. I heard you talking on the bus about living in the east."

"We are from there. At least me and my family are. You?" Guy asked.

"I am. I have family in New York. I was out here for an audition."

Ruben looked over to Guy when he heard the words 'New York'.

Abby continued, "Hopefully I can get close to home. And maybe, like I said, you have a plan?"

"We don't," Ruben said. "I believe we will soon." He pulled the radio from the back of his pocket. "I grabbed fresh batteries. With any luck I can pick something up."

"I saw the look between you two, I can go somewhere else," Abby said. "Another part of the airport if you don't want me to stay."

"No." Guy rolled out the word. "Don't be silly. That look was because we just … we heard things didn't go well out east. They were hit, too." He reached out and grabbed her arm. "You are welcome to join us. Go where we go. Stay where we stay."

"Thank you."

"I have blankets," Ruben said. "Help yourself. It's getting cold."

"Or you can stand by the fire," Guy suggested. "I'm going out there for a bit. Carter?"

"Can I sit on the bench by the window?" Carter asked.

"Sure can. Stay where I can see you." Guy pointed.

"I'll be in here," Abby said. "I'll make sure he doesn't run off."

"Much obliged," Guy said, kissed his grandson and then walked through the open doors.

"How did we not see her?" Ruben asked as he stepped out.

"Poor thing was probably scared to approach us. Felt like maybe she intruded. I don't know. Do we look unfriendly?"

"You didn't until you changed out of that mouse t-shirt."

Guy smiled, then the smile dropped from his face as he stared out.

"You alright?"

"Yeah," Guy grumbled. "Just worried. No sign of them. It's night. They left right after us. Where are they?"

"It's conceivable they had to walk. If they walked they probably stopped."

"Walked?" Guy asked. "My God there was a wave coming."

"Yeah, but think about it. It was a tsunami right? We saw them at the convention center. They were already twenty-five or so miles from the shore. Another couple miles they had to be safe from the wave. They got out. They just had to walk. I believe it," Ruben said. "After all, realistically how far could that wave have really washed in?"

"Fifty-five miles roughly," Gary explained to Parker and Charles.

"What about the East Coast?" Parker asked.

"About thirty miles. This isn't a wave, this isn't something that is going to recede, this is the new coastline. The Atlantic didn't get hit as hard as the Pacific. They estimated one of the rocks that landed in the Pacific to be about two and a half miles in diameter. That wave is still rolling in toward the west.

"Two miles?"" Parker asked in shocked. "My God, the one that hit sixty-five million years ago was six miles. It wiped out the dinosaurs."

"Yeah, in like twenty thousand years," Gary replied. "Extinctions don't happen overnight. We'll be long gone and this extinction event will still be happening."

"But it's done? Everything is over, right?" Charles asked.

Gary shook his head. "Two more are due with-in the next hour. One will strike the west coast of Australia, the other somewhere in

Northern Africa. The Russians are pretty good with their data. They're working as hard as they can and are up and running."

"Of course." Parker tossed his hands up. "They haven't been hit."

"Well, they have. They weren't spared, they just got hit in places that really didn't make a big difference. It's not a bad thing," Gary said. "They are doing their part of reconnecting the world, doing what they can. Helping out where they can. Unfortunately … or fortunately, depending on how you want to look at it, they are the only functioning power globally right now. They're trying their hardest to get information out to everyone."

"What about our imaging?" Charles asked. "Have you seen it?"

"They're working on getting connections up enough to send them," Gary said. "They're hopeful by morning we'll have something. However, you need to know, they told me thermal imaging is showing Yellowstone will go, as well. At least one vent."

"One vent will be all it takes," said Charles.

Gary nodded. "Right here. Where we are, between Long Valley and Yellowstone, we're looking at a foot or two of heavy ash. Problem isn't just the ash, yes, that's a problem. We need to also worry about what goes up comes down. The ocean impacts blasted water into the atmosphere. You have dirt, debris and ash all up in the stratosphere, as it comes down, it will combine with the gases from the volcanic eruption, mixing up a storm with rain that will be deadly to plant, animal life you name it. From about Chicago to the West coast."

"Oh my God," Parker exclaimed.

"What do we do?" Charles asked. "Where do people go?"

"We have to do our damnedest to get the Emergency Alert system running. Advise people of the dangers, I'll get a list together of them. Let them know what to do. Those migrating from west of the Rockies need to head south before heading east. Those on the East Coast or near to it, can't stay there," Gary said. "There's increased risk of more tsunamis. Safe zones would be east of

Indianapolis, but no further north than Toronto, and no further east than Pittsburgh."

"Jesus, you want me to cram four hundred million Americans into maybe ten percent of the country?" Parker asked.

"Begging you pardon, sir, when this is all said and done, and even before the last catastrophe hits," Gary said. "There will be nowhere near four hundred million Americans to move."

TWENTY-TWO

"Never thought I'd see the day when I could hear the ocean three miles away from San Bernardino," a man said not far from where CJ sat by a small fire.

He never really gave much thought to how far inland they were, nor the fact that the water from the tsunami remained constant. He did, after hearing the man say that.

However, the subtle wave sounds were not the only things CJ heard. He could hear clanking and crashing as items rolled about in the water.

They had finally made it through the water. But the severely overcast sky blocked out most of the daylight and it started to get extremely dark. They needed to use what little light they had left to salvage for supplies to get them through the night. Once the evening fully moved in, it was total blackness outside. The only semblance of light they had was the still red, glowing horizon.

There was a chill in the air, and CJ was only warm when he stayed close to the heat of the fire.

But the man's comment about hearing the ocean made CJ think. He stood and walked towards the water. It wasn't that far, maybe fifty feet. He couldn't see it, but he could hear and smell it. CJ followed that until he saw the reflection off the beam from his small pen light.

It wasn't reflecting off the water, however, it reflected off the fog or steam.

He crouched down and touched for the water. His hand blindly reached through the fog or steam until he felt the water. It was warm, like bath water. With the lower temperatures in the air around it, the steam now made sense.

Like a little kid only allowed on the edge, CJ kept moving his hand in the water playing with it. He didn't know why he continued, perhaps it was something mindless to occupy himself with.

"Worried about Carter?" Mindy's voice came from behind him.

"Huh?" CJ registered what she asked and stood up. "No. No, I'm not. He's with my father. What's going on?"

"I saw you. I was worried?"

"Saw me? Boy you must have good eyes." He lifted the light to shine on her face.

Mindy squinted. "What the hell?"

"Looking at you. Can you please rest? There are some cars. You can get in one of those."

"I'm fine."

"No, you're not." CJ took her arm and walked back toward his fire. "Will you at least sit with me?"

"Yes, I will."

"Did you eat anything?" He led her by the fire.

"Not much. Apparently someone must have been snack mom for the week at little league. Found a bunch for snacks and stuff. I passed them out."

"You forgot about me," CJ said.

"I'm sorry." She sat down. "I can find more."

"No. You need to stop. You shouldn't have been looking around. How's your stomach?"

"My belly. My stomach's fine, I injured my belly. Like I said, it must have happened when I squeezed out the window. I'll be fine." She looked down at the fire. "You have a new bag," she said and pointed.

"I do. And look what else I found …" he opened the bag and pulled out a pint of whiskey. "This will hit the spot just about now." He uncapped it, brought it to his lips and paused. "Oh, shit. Sorry." He pulled it away. "I remember reading somewhere that you don't drink and don't allow anyone to drink around you."

"You go on. It's fine. I did have a problem, a bad one," she said. "I hit the rock bottom of the rock bottom. That was six years ago, I have been sober ever since."

"That's great. I won't drink."

"I'm fine, really. I can be around it. The whole 'no booze' rule was for Raf. My lead dancer. He had issues and needed to stay clean. For himself, his wife and his little girl." Mindy brought her legs close to her chest and wrapped her arms around them. "I can handle it. I just didn't want him to have to handle it."

"That was nice."

"I loved Raf. I hope … I hope he made it. I hope he got out of there and is headed home. His family needs him."

"What about you? Any family that needs you?" CJ asked.

"My mom passed away last year. She was all I had. That and a slew of ex-husbands, three of which need my alimony." She laughed. "I was so stupid. Never did a prenup. I don't know what they would have done if I died that night. Then again, one of them I wouldn't have married if I had died."

"Was that the rock bottom of the rock bottom?" CJ asked.

"Yep. Ruben saved my life, you know. If it wasn't for him, I'd be dead. The doctors said that. In fact, he broke my manager's number one rule. He was supposed to not even look back at me. I think because he didn't understand English very well that he didn't know about the rules. Thank God."

"Oh, Thank … wait." CJ looked at her. "Ruben didn't understand English six years ago?"

Mindy nodded. "He's come a long way."

"I heard him speak. He doesn't have a lick of an accent."

"Nope." Mindy shook his head. "He is really good now. Still once and awhile he goes quiet, but I made it my goal to make sure he knows the language. He's with me a lot. I hope his son is okay. He has a son in college. In Texas. I'm sure Ruben is worried."

"I'm sure," CJ said.

"I'm glad you aren't worried about Carter anymore."

"I mean, I worry about him. But I am sure he's fine. Like I said, he's with my dad. My dad raised me. You can't ask for a better protector."

"What about your mom?" Mindy asked.

"She passed when I was little."

"And Carter's mom?"

CJ looked down to the bottle and took a drink. "We broke up when Carter was two."

"I'm sorry."

"Don't be. She has a great life now. One I was never able to give her. I'm an independent painter, so I was working job to job, you know."

"Oh, a painter, How wonderful. A painter like Van Gogh, Picasso? DaVinci?"

"No, a painter like Sherwin Williams."

"I'm not familiar with his work."

"It's a brand of paint. I paint houses."

"That's still artistic."

CJ smiled. "In a way. But I like to be my own boss, sort of like my dad was. He worked as a handyman for hire. I guess Kylie … that's Carter's mom, couldn't take it. She left. If you asked me five years ago, I would have said I was blindsided, but time gives a different perspective. I wasn't home, and when I was, I wasn't there. Money was up and down. We were together for so long, it was like … I stopped seeing her, you know?"

Mindy nodded. "I do."

"But … she's happy. She got married again, the guy is good to my son."

"Are you going to try to find her?" Mindy asked.

"Nope."

"Wait. That was fast. You're not gonna try to find the mother of your son?"

"It's not my problem. My son is my concern. She's not my wife. If she wants to find Carter, she'll look. I'll make sure we leave his name wherever we go. It's not my place to look for his mother. It's my place to keep him safe. Realistically I won't find her in all this mayhem. I'm not going to put my son at risk to do so. I just want to find a safe place for him."

"What about what Carter wants?"

"I'm sure he wants his mom. I'm sure all kids do. But I can't look for her when I am looking after his best interests."

Mindy nodded with an 'hmm.'

"What? What was that for?"

"You talk real tough. But you wanna know what I think? I think in that mind of yours, she's never far and you're already trying to figure out how to get them two together."

"You're wrong."

"I could be. I don't think I am."

"How do you know?" CJ asked.

"Because you really are a nice person." After she said that she grimaced and ran her hand over her abdomen.

"What's wrong?"

Mindy shook her head. "Just a little discomfort. But I am going to try to find a car to sleep. Will you be alright?"

CJ lifted his pint. "I'm be fine."

"Good night, CJ."

"Good night." He watched Mindy stand and then walk off. She seemed to know exactly where she would go, walking directly toward a blue minivan.

After she was out of his sight, CJ lifted the bottle again. He looked at the flames of his fire through the brown liquid and took another sip.

He needed to conserve, it was all he had to make it through the night. It was going to be a long night. CJ didn't plan on sleeping. He didn't want to take a chance on something happening.

Daylight wouldn't be that far away. And though the night seemed as if it would be long, CJ thought about the next day and how after they started walking, it wouldn't be long at all until he was with his son.

TWENTY-THREE

"Merry Christmas! It's Christmas!"

Guy knew where the dream came from. Just after he had the deli sandwich and before he settled for the night, he found a Good Housekeeping magazine. The woman on the front wore a gaudy, green, Christmas tree sweater, with the words, 'Fast Holiday meals for last minute guests'.

It made him think about the time he planned on spending Christmas, just him, with Guy and Carter. Carter was four, excited about Santa, and it was CJ's holiday turn.

Then shortly after CJ showed up for Christmas Eve dinner, and right before Guy put the fish on the table, Kylie showed up.

He should have seen it coming. She was neurotic and anxious, and with the death of her mother six months earlier, Kylie was out of sorts. She had begged CJ to not take Carter. Guy heard them on the phone and yelled in the back. "Christ, just tell her to come over.'

He guessed she heard it because Kylie did. It ended up being a nice Christmas. She brought him a present, a bag of weed she bought from an undisclosed source. That memory started an enormous chain reaction, leading Guy on a search after Carter had fallen asleep.

Assured by Ruben he'd keep watch until Guy returned, he headed to TSA where he hit the marijuana jackpot.

Those vapor pens confiscated at checkpoint. Guy found three of them. After the previous two days he had he needed it, he really enjoyed his vape of weed by the fire.

When the fire died down, Guy slipped inside and was able to rest. He fell fast and hard asleep, dreaming about Christmas and Carter running about announcing to everyone the holiday had arrived.

Until he realized it wasn't a dream and Carter's voice woke him up.

"It's Christmas!" Carter yelled. "Pap, get up. Hurry. It's Christmas. It's snowing. If it sticks can we make a snow man?'

Snow in California?

Guy sat up. He didn't dismiss it. After all the temperature had dropped after the series of events.

At this point, anything was possible. He swung his legs over the bench, sat up and scratched his head. He hadn't been asleep long, he knew that.

Just when he focused he saw Ruben and another man closing the sliding glass doors. A few blinks of his eyes and sure as hell he saw the flakes tumbling from the sky.

He stood and staggered over toward Ruben.

"Now I've seen it all," Guy said. "It's snowing in San Bernardino."

"Look again." Ruben told him. "It's ash."

CJ didn't sleep. He was up all night. Awake enough to watch what people did and to listen to conversations, to their tears and even some laughter.

One thing resonated among them, a single, simple question, "Then what?"

It was asked in reference to the decision they all had to follow CJ to the airport.

Get to the airport … then what?

A part of CJ didn't care, he didn't invite them along. He certainly didn't have any answers for them at all.

He, himself, couldn't even answer the 'then what' question. Because he didn't know. He just didn't know. He hoped his father had answers, maybe knew more than he did. After all, his father was on a bus, perhaps the drivers knew more about the situation.

He watched the sky a lot, the threatening red looked less scary as the sky lightened. It didn't lighten too much.

The clouds were a deep, dark gray, some were even downright black. The temperature had dropped enough his Raynaud's disease flared up. That usually only happened in temps less than sixty. His fingertips went numb and white. CJ warmed them in the water.

Finally, it seemed everyone slept. Everyone but CJ. He watched the time, ready to go as soon as it was light enough.

When that happened when he felt they could move on, he snuffed his fire, grabbed his stuff and headed to the car where Mindy slept. He wanted to wake her, make sure she was alright. He was still the only one awake, and the first one to feel and see the ash fall.

CJ didn't know at first what it was, he even considered the possibility of snow. It began with a few flakes, then the light gray matter fell from the sky rapidly within minutes.

CJ caught it in his hand. He knew upon first sight that it was ash. He didn't need to rub his fingers through it. He did, though. It was rough and coarse.

"Everyone!" CJ hollered out. "Hey, wake up and cover up."

"What's going on?" Someone asked.

CJ was just about to answer when someone else did.

"It's ash. I think it's ash."

"It is," said another.

"What the hell erupted?"

Erupted? CJ didn't even think on those terms. He thought something was burning and they were getting the ash. Whatever caused it, CJ was at least smart enough to know, walking and breathing in the ash wasn't a good thing.

He opened the car door and Mindy was stirring.

"Hey," he said.

"What's going on?" she cringed as she sat up.

"You doing alright?'

"I feel horrible. But I'll be fine, we only have a couple miles, right."

"Right. And we need to move. Ash is falling."

Mindy didn't ask about it, she merely tilted her head with a questioning look.

"We have to move," CJ said.

Mindy nodded.

After stepping back to give her privacy, CJ urged everyone to gather their things quickly. As Mindy said, it was only a couple miles. Which was a good thing because the shortest time they were out in the falling ash, the better.

Cheyenne Mountain, Colorado

"It blew."

No 'good morning Mr. President.' Or 'We need to speak to you'. When Parker opened his eyes after a few hours rest, he looked up to see Charles.

"It blew," Charles said.

Not exactly the scientific or technical term he expected to hear, but 'it blew' summed it all up.

"We expected one vent," Gary explained in the morning meeting. "Russia contacted us this morning. Seems three vents erupted and they are expecting that the images they are sending this afternoon will be one of the last clear shots of the US. They are hoping to give us an idea where and how far the cloud will travel."

"I've seen the projections," Parker said. "Those Yellowstone ash maps have been around forever. I'm aware. Just … just like I am aware that we are not in a good area."

"No, we are not," Gary said. "The ash has already started to fall here. Within twelve hours there will be so much ash, travel will be impossible. If it falls like I predict, and then rain, we can be looking at never getting out of here."

"Impossible," Parker said. "This place is designed to be able to evacuate under any circumstance."

"Mr. President, I don't think this was designed with a super volcano in mind."

"Well we have far too many people to evacuate."

"This is true. Now the good news ..."

"There's good news?" Parker asked.

"Yes." Gary nodded. "The good news is we have more than one vent blowing its top."

"How is that good news?"

"Look at it this way," Gary said. "If you have a hole in the bottom of a cup and you put water in it, it's gonna take a lot longer to drip out if you have three holes in it."

"My God, what is it with you and analogies? Parker asked.

"I like analogies. And I am just saying. The eruption won't go on as long. In my opinion," Gary said. "It is also my opinion you should initiate a partial evacuation. Take as many people and supplies as you can in a truck and leave a team who knows we're here, who can come back and get us."

Charles looked at Parker. "We do this now, pack a truck, take the twelve children we have and the adults with them, and go."

"Where?" Parker asked.

"The closest, safest point from here ... Midland, Texas," Gary replied.

"Just like that? Midland. Did you pull that out of a hat or is there science behind it?" Parker asked.

"I'm basing this on ash projection maps and knowledge," Gary said. "We know the ash cloud from both Long Valley and Yellowstone will carry east. Interstate 40 is a great gauging line. Everything south of there should be free from heavy ash, at least enough to make a difference. We know a meteor hit twenty-two miles south of Dallas. It activated the Balcones Fault which triggered quakes in excess of eight points on the Richter scale in the Houston, San Antonio area. Midland is your biggest point of contact in a safe zone. We are trying to reach FEMA in those areas."

"Is FEMA even up and running?" Parker asked.

"Not FEMA as we know. But we have managed to make contact with some areas that aren't as bad off, some small towns and cities. We are trying to nail down locations that are willing to help refugees or injured."

"I'm sure that's everywhere," Parker said.

Charles shook his head. "Some just don't want to use their resources on refugees. We're trying to get supplies to them. And we will …" Charles added. "Have the Emergency Alert system or a variation of it, up and running in about two hours. We're recording the loop now and we're going to send the signal until we can't because of the ash."

"And you think sending out a small group is best?" Parker asked. "I just can't see that, considering we have everything we need here."

"Except a way out," Gary said. "If it all turns to stone. What good is surviving if we're stuck in here?"

"I still don't believe that," Parker said, standing up. "But let's get the children out and somewhere that is definitely safe. We will also divide the government, which is you and me," he said to Charles. "That way we aren't putting all our leadership eggs in one basket."

"So I'm going with the convoy?" Charles asked.

"Yes. Get things in motion. In the meantime, I'll keep trying FEMA and work on safe stops for those migrating. There are a lot of people out there who need our help," Parker said. "Let's do our best to get it to them."

TWENTY-FOUR

The blue plastic, drug store shopping carts were a godsend. So were the items in the store. Aside from candy, snacks and drinks, they loaded carts with other items they needed. One such item was protective facial masks. They were the thick round ones, but they worked, covering noses and mouths to prevent breathing in the ash.

Items also helped Rose.

Using things they picked up there they lined the cart to give it cushion and placed Rose inside. She slept comfortably and didn't speak much. She wasn't well. Marty pushed the cart, maneuvering around any broken concrete or things that got in his way. He stopped letting people help him, he wanted to do it on his own.

There wasn't a single medical professional in the group. Which seemed unusual to CJ. Anytime he was in a crowd, it seemed there was always at least one nurse in the midst.

No one knew exactly what was wrong with Rose, but it was obvious she sustained injuries in the crash. Injuries that left her listless and nearly comatose. A lot of people were injured, many of them saying it was when the wave wiped out their vehicle. The bandages and pain medication from the drug store did very little. They were weak, fighting to move on. CJ started to believe that Mindy was one of the injured.

She claimed she scraped or bumped her belly getting out of the car when it was underwater, but she increasingly looked drawn and pale. She moved slowly, which was unlike her and she started to stagger in her walk.

He knew something was up when he woke her. She inched her way out of the car, arm draped over her abdomen.

Yet, if he asked her, she stated she was fine and just tired. He even offered to get her a drug store cart and push her.

Mindy said, "Don't be silly. I can walk."

And she did, but her pace was slow and CJ stayed right by her.

Slow was good, though. The falling ash was like snow, giving everything a light covering. The city was barren. Not a soul was around, nor did they see a car. It was a ghost town.

By the looks of things the citizens just moved on.

"We're almost there," CJ said.

"Have you thought about the 'then what'?" she asked.

CJ had an answer. An answer he didn't want to give. 'Yeah,' he thought. 'find somewhere, somehow, where's there's medical attention. You need it.' But he didn't say that. He simply replied, "No. I'm hoping my father has it all figured out."

"Have you always left it up to your father?"

"You don't know my father," CJ said. "He doesn't leave me much of a choice."

"I wish I knew my father," she said almost breathless. "I didn't. I always wondered if he knew about me. If he knew he had a child."

"What did your mother say?"

"I never asked her." Mindy paused and looked down.

"What's wrong?"

"Just tired," she said.

"Wanna take a break?"

"No … no. We need to get out of this ash. It's not too far. It can't be."

It really couldn't have been far. CJ saw signs, they were so close. But the group of two dozen people pushing their carts, the injured staggering, moved so slowly it could have been a hundred miles.

They trudged on. The leg of the journey would be complete when they arrived at the airport.

Unfortunately, CJ realized it wouldn't be their last stop. With Rose, the other injured and Mindy, CJ knew finding medical help would be the first priority. If they didn't, the group two dozen strong would probably be a third of that in a few days.

The map was pretty and had topography. It probably wasn't meant to be any more than a souvenir, but Abby believed it exceeded her expectations. She found it in a frame in the lounge of the private terminal a half a block away. The only reason she knew it was there, or hoped it was there, was she saw it in a pamphlet at the welcome counter. The image was of two private pilots having a drink at the bar, in the back on the wall was the map.

When the ash fell, she ventured over there.

Sure enough, there it was.

She grabbed that, a first aid kit and a bottle of vodka. She wasn't a drinker, this was for medicinal purposes. Her knowledge of first aid was limited. However, her knowledge of the map was not. After finding a highlighter , she worked on the map then headed back to the main terminal.

"By tomorrow," she said pointing down to the map. "We'll be covered with an inch or two of ash. Far less than that is needed to close an airport."

"This here you have circled?" Guy asked. "What is this?"

"The area getting the heaviest ash from the eruption."

"Eruption of what?"

"A super volcano," she replied.

"Super volcano?" Guy laughed. "You think a super volcano erupted?"

"You act like you don't believe there's a super volcano."

He shook his head.

Ruben interjected. "They are real. Where have you been? Yellowstone? You never head …"

"Ah, yeah, yeah." Guy nodded then snapped his finger. "I heard of that. So you think Yellowstone erupted?

"I don't know about Yellowstone, but I think Long Valley did."

"I never heard of that. It can't be that big," Guy said.

"The comparison I was given is if Mount St. Helens is a raisin, then Long Valley is an apple and Yellowstone is a bagel."

Guy was rendered speechless, in fact all he could do was clear his throat.

"Ash will continue to fall, because the volcano will continue to erupt, sometimes for weeks. It will move east."

"How do you know it's this … Long Valley," Guy said, waving about his hand. "And not Yellowstone."

"We wouldn't get this much ash if it were Yellowstone."

"How do we know it was a volcano at all?" Ruben questioned. "Just asking. I mean we had a shit load of meteors fall from the sky. It could be ash from things burning."

"Could be." Abby shook her head. "I'm positive it isn't. The meteors are what caused it. I think. Chain reaction, they were already on the cusp of eruption."

"So what do we do?" Guy asked,

"Right now, cover our mouths and get supplies. We need to head out. South. Outside these areas, if we leave tomorrow, then we won't run into much problem."

"Traveling across country to those areas sounds good," Guy said. "Even if we find a vehicle, how the hell will we go very far? I'm pretty sure the gas stations will be closed."

Ruben snapped his finger. "Diesel. There …" he stepped back. "There is the diesel tank truck they were using to fuel the buses on the airfield. The toy shipment center is across the street. There are a lot of trucks. We will take one and follow with the tanker."

"That's saying the ash keeps falling like snow. That's saying it was a volcanic eruption." Guy said. "I'm still not convinced."

The sudden flash of light and clap of thunder outside the terminal window caused them to look and walk that way.

"Would ash from a fire do that?" Abby pointed. "There is so much debris and movement in the ash clouds it's causing lightning.

God help us if it rains."

"Wow." Guy said. "Here I thought you were an actress."

"I am."

"But a scientist, right? A teacher?"

"No, an actress," Abby replied. "I mean I did work at the news station."

"As a weather woman?" Guy asked.

"No, a teleprompter writer."

"No scientific knowledge, education, whatsoever?" Guy asked. "How do you know any of this?"

"I was in a docudrama on Yellowstone," she said. "I played a scientist."

Guy stared at her and blinked.

"Do you know how many times I did this exact same scene, convincing others of what was on the way? It's just so weird," she said. "No one yelling 'cut', I did kind of stumble over the ash cloud stuff."

Guy just stared.

"What?" she asked, "Everything I said was based on scientific fact."

"In a movic."

"Um … a docudrama and not just any docudrama, it was on the Science Channel Network."

"Oh that makes it better."

"Hey, Guy," Ruben moved more toward the window. "Either we're being attacked by a hoard of bargain shoppers or your son has arrived and brought people."

Guy ran over to the window. Not far away, was a large group. It was hard to see, they looked like shadows. He could see that some pushed shopping carts, they all moved slowly.

Guy pried the sliding door open enough to step out. He ignored Abby who cautioned him to cover his mouth, and he raced out to the driveway.

The ash fell as fast as any snow storm Guy had experienced and the wind whipped viciously, blowing it around as the continuous flashes of lightning made everything look ominous and grim.

It was a world without color, only a dozen shades of gray.

Guy didn't want to believe some super volcano erupted, but being out in it, seeing how it intensified, Guy couldn't deny it any longer.

He watched the group approach and prayed his son was among them.

Cheyenne Mountain, Colorado

Lieutenant Colonel Stefan Rush had been at Cheyenne Mountain for a while, months actually, it was his home. He was second in command on base, the Executive Office, and he had ended up taking the reins when the General was called to Washington a week before the events.

Had the meteors not arrived, Rush was as close to being relieved of duty as one could come. He was labeled nuts and out of control. Now he wasn't even able to say 'I told you so'.

As a portion of the globe prepared to watch the greatest lightshow as the meteor shower approached, Rush and his men monitored the air and sea around the continental United States.

He wasn't quite sure how the information ended up on his desk. It was a one of those instances where a friend of the brother of one of his top communication specialist brought it to his attention. The 'friend' was an amateur astronomer, who relayed it to the brother who told the specialist … forty percent of those meteors expected to be only lights in the sky were asteroids with several being extinction level size.

Rush wouldn't have taken it so seriously had his specialist not insisted that the astronomer wasn't some crack pot.

When the would be sky watcher sent the images to Rush, he included a note that said, "Yes, the dark side of the globe will see a hell of a light show, but we on this side of the earth will witness the end of world. They are that big."

Then the note went on to ask if they could send some missiles out there.

Rush forwarded the information. While he didn't understand the measurements and data the kid included, someone in Washington did. No one paid it any attention. Or maybe they did, and the fact that it was only twenty-four hours before the event someone figured 'why bother'.

Rush took flack for not only sending the information and wasting time, but for receiving and sending what was considered personal email on a classified server.

"We will speak when I return," the general told him.

Something inside of Rush was unsettled, the information just scared him a little. So much so, that, figuring what the hell, he was already in trouble, he used his connection and a dedicated line at base to contact NASA, and pretty much … lied about the information.

Time was of the essence and there wasn't much time left.

"We think we discovered something here," Rush told them. "Can we send the information your way?"

Oddly, NASA had a man named Gary Boothe not fifty miles away speaking to students who planned to watch the light show.

Rush got him clearance and Gary arrived. Gary didn't dismiss the discover. He immediately got on the phone and NASA began their own calculations. Unfortunately it was only hours until impact when everything was confirmed. Only enough time to get the president out.

Since that moment, Rush had done nothing but get things ready. Send out trucks, pick up supplies, pack the trucks that may be needed to go out to aid people. Nothing went as planned. Things went awry with the wave. His efforts had to be maxed out and amped up when the eruptions occurred. Rush wasn't planning on the need to evacuate the entire states of California, Washington and Oregon. Now he had to add several others to that as well. Nevada, Iowa and Wyoming.

Everything changed, including his goals. He worked non-stop on building communications, reaching out, helping the president come up with a viable plan. When of course the president listened.

The president was a good guy, down to earth, but Rush thought he was a bit spacy.

He reviewed his most recent orders on things to prepare and that didn't mesh with what he had in mind. The president's plan would not work with all that was happening, and Rush had to tell him.

For the first two days, Rush was buried in the communications room, speaking only to those he worked with and communicating with the president via a man named Charles.

That had to change.

There would be no chance of miscommunication and Rush requested to speak to the president.

"Thank you for meeting with me, sir," Rush said. "I appreciate you taking the time."

"What's going on?"

"Sir, we are facing the possibility of being buried under three feet of ash. With the storms that are predicted, personnel and survivors remaining may have to move to the entrances and the tunnels that lead to the heliports, because we stand a chance of losing our air filtering system."

"Should we all evacuate?"

"I would think it was wise to move those we can, if we didn't need this facility to command I'd say we all leave. I do advise you leave with the Chief of Staff. You can't and shouldn't govern under three feet of ash."

"This is the only place still standing on this side of the county that has the technology to command, I can't leave Colonel, I appreciate your concern," Parker said. "I'll stay and weather it out. Anything else?"

"I have taken the liberty of initiating refugee centers and have informed them to register names as they pass through. Even if they want just a cup of water, get a name," Rush said. "There are a lot of people coming from the west that have a lot of family worried about them. We need a way for people to locate each other."

"Agreed," Parker said.

"We can't guarantee efficiency or quality at this point. We are just getting things up as fast as we can. Also, we are preparing a rescue and surveillance truck. I will be dispatching that truck south to monitor Interstate 10. I have that scheduled to leave within the hour."

"Can I ask why *that* highway."

"The shaking has stopped, meteors are finished and the ash is filling the sky. Right now we have people leaving six states with nowhere to go. We have to give them direction. We have to give them a destination or we're going to have chaos."

"FEMA is working on that."

"FEMA isn't doing much right now. We managed to get ahold of the Texas Emergency Response and they are sending an expedited medical set up to the Tucson city limits.

"Why isn't Arizona handling that?"

"They are not accepting refugees, sir. Travelers will be rejected. That is why we are setting up the camp right now as we speak. There are reports of massive civil unrest in Phoenix."

"That's insane."

"Yes, well, it's not good. Communications, at least radio, are up and reports aren't good. That's another reason we need to give refugees a destination. We have the Emergency Alert system ready to start. We are going to broadcast at the strongest signal we can, trying to reach every radio big and small. We have divided destination cities by state. "

Parker paced back and forth. "We are supposed to come together at a time like this. Why is this the first time I am hearing about it?"

"Because prior to this morning, the only true communication we had was with Russia and a man in Mammoth Mountain. We are moving as fast as we can."

"I appreciate it." Parker nodded. "Do what you feel needs to be done, Colonel, get that rescue truck out? If we can spare it, get another truck with survivors."

"Yes, sir."

Parker walked toward the exit. "Thank you again."

After the president left, Rush immediately returned to his tasks. He would give his all and do all that he could, but he was limited and realistic. It wasn't just part of the country affected, it was the entire world. He wasn't sure that a few refugee centers would cut it in the long run. The chaos in Phoenix and other cities were just the beginning. He feared anything they did would be like putting a Band-Aid on a gunshot wound. Without a permanent fix, humanity, just like that wound would eventually bleed out.

It was like Christmas in July, only a lot more gray.

Parker stood at the western opening of the mountain. It was higher than ground level, about three stories, and it led to a manmade cliff used for helicopters.

That heliport was covered with ash that swirled with the winds. The sky was dark gray and the fast moving clouds flashed with lightning as large clumps of ash dropped from above.

What happened to the world?

In everyone's mind, whether fear or fascination, at some point, they envisioned the end. A doomsday scenario. Never would Parker have believed he would be facing something that had never crossed his mind.

"You need to cover your nose and mouth," Charles said. "Eyes, too."

"I'm not out there." Parker turned and looked at Charles who did wear a facemask and pair of goggles.

"You're still breathing it in."

"Look at it," Parker said. "This is horrible."

"That's putting it mildly."

"Are you scared of going out in this?"

"Can I be honest? I'm more scared of staying. This is only going to get worse. It's going to fall and keep on falling."

"And it's still the beginning."

"Excuse me."

Parker faced Charles. "I didn't want to believe it. I was inside seeing none of this. My view of the world was a few satellite images sent from the Russians. Now … now it's real. I see how truly this is the beginning of the end. You know, we sit in there, and we talk about long term. We draw blanks, we say, 'let's wait until the dust settles, see where we are'. The dust, my friend, will never settle. What we do right now, in the immediate is all we can do."

"That's not true."

"Yes, it is and you know it. There is no long term. There is no aid coming from overseas, there are no celebrities getting together to sing a song. It's not just here, it's everywhere. And this …" Parker pointed to the sky. "And every other thing that's happened, the dust and ash will circle the globe. I read what Gary wrote, but I didn't want to believe it. Temperatures will drop, pretty much the next ice age, we'll lose seventy percent of crops, water will become polluted, and in six months, we as the government will have exhausted every resource we have to give. We'll have to stop because we won't have anything to help them with."

"Then why are we doing this?" Charles asked. "If it's such a futile attempt."

"Like the Colonel told me, we need to give people direction. Give them hope, and maybe, just maybe they can hold on to that when they're on their own. Sooner or later, it will be every man for himself. And if we think the world is bad now," Parker said. "God help us all then."

TWENTY-FIVE

CJ knew it, because CJ knew his father well. They were fine. Better than him, Mindy and the others.

The moment he saw his father standing outside of the terminal door, he raced forward, swept his son into his arms and embraced his father.

Covered in ash, CJ knew the reunion had to be short lived.

A woman he didn't know was with his father, and ushered everyone inside, urging them to take advantage of the running water and wash as much ash as they could from their skin. She also stated there was plenty of abandoned luggage and for them to search out clean and dry clothes.

CJ knew that was a good idea. His skin burned from irritation, and even though he wore that facemask, it was caked with ash and he started to cough.

Mindy tried to put on a good front. She showed enthusiasm when she met Guy and Carter, then shrieked in relief upon seeing Ruben.

Then she quickly excused herself to go get cleaned up.

"It's bad out there, Dad," CJ said. "Getting worse by the minute."

"Abby there," Guy pointed. "Says it was some sort of super volcano eruption and this isn't going to stop."

"Do you think it's safe here?" CJ asked.

Before Guy could answer, Abby, who was walking by, paused and interjected. "No. The ash is heavy. The roof will collapse before long, that's if it doesn't rain first."

"Thank you, Greta Garbo," Guy said.

"We talked about the trucks," Ruben said. "The tanker and getting a truck. We could get on that now."

"Head out in the morning?" Guy asked.

"No." Abby replied. "Who knows how much ash will fall by

then. We already run the risk of clogging up the engines. Our best bet is to go as soon as possible."

Guy sighed out. "You have an answer for everything."

"I'm just trying to help."

"When do you propose we leave then?" Guy asked. "It's not even noon and dark out there. It's gonna take a few hours to get the trucks and these folks ready. We'll be driving at night before long, then we won't see anything. The ash is bad enough and dangerous."

"We stop," Ruben suggested. "We get things ready, we go and we stop when we can't see. We should go get the tanker and the truck."

"Alright, I'll go," Guy said.

"Or me," CJ said. "I can help."

"No. Stay here, CJ, you need to get cleaned up. Guy … just stay put." Ruben replied. "Abby, do you want to go with me? Can you drive one of those?"

"I played a truck driver once in a crime show."

"Christ," Guy grumbled.

"We'll be back," Ruben said, "In the meantime, get everyone situated and informed."

Guy nodded.

CJ couldn't help but chuckle at his father's irritation. After Ruben and the woman walked away, he ran his hand over Carter's head and then faced his dad. "I'm going to go get cleaned up. I won't be long."

"We'll try to find you some clothes," Guy said.

"Thanks." CJ stepped away. "I'm glad you guys are okay."

"Dad?" Carter called out. "I drowned. I died and everything, ask pap."

CJ stopped walking.

"Oh, stop," Guy said. "You're exaggerating. He's exaggerating. Go get cleaned up."

CJ smiled and hurried off.

"Now, why would you say that?" Guy asked Carter. "We can

save that for later."

"I'm glad he's okay and with us."

"Yeah." Guy pulled Carter to him. "Me, too."

The oversized Cal U sweatshirt was in a rose colored carry on, left at gate four. Mindy found it, took it to wear, but before she placed it on, she covered her mouth, to block out the noise, and sobbed in a bathroom stall.

There were many reasons why she cried. She tried to put on a great front, a strong front, but she was folding inside, not to mention, she knew something was wrong with her body. She literally could not go on anymore, and couldn't be happier they were finally stopping. She took a while getting cleaned up, but she felt emotionally and physically better when she left the women's room.

As she walked out, intent on looking for Ruben or CJ, she saw Marty at Gate Two.

He crouched on the floor by a connected row of seats. Rose lay on those seats, eyes closed while Marty wiped her face. Neither looked like they had done anything but just sit down. Marty was still covered in ash.

She walked over to the couple.

"Hey," she said gently. "I can watch her if you want to go change clothes or clean up."

"No." He shook his head. "I'm fine."

"Marty, we're going to be leaving soon. We have to get out of the area. Maybe we can find some help for her."

"We aren't going, Mindy. Don't worry about us."

"Of course, we do. We all do. If we get Rose to a doctor, they can help her."

"My dear," he spoke softly. "She's in God's hands now."

"Marty, I know you …" Mindy's voice trailed off when she

realized what he meant. She reached out her finger tips, touching them softly to Rose's face. Her skin was cold and hard. "Oh, Marty, I am so sorry."

"I am, too."

"We can take her with us. Take her so we can give her a proper burial."

"No. I'm not going."

"If you stay behind, you will die."

Marty only raised his eyes.

"Marty, please."

"I spent fifty-two years married to this woman. Life isn't life without her."

Mindy's lips pursed in sadness when she heard him say that. "Okay. If you need me, I'll be right over there."

"Thank you."

She gently grazed her hand over his as she walked away. Ten feet was all she moved and the sharp pains began again in her abdomen. She sat down by the windows with a heavy sigh.

She needed a rest, just a short rest, she prepared to close her eyes when Ruben came to her.

Mindy smiled.

He sat next to her and glanced out the window. "Good view?"

"Yes, it is. It looks like snow."

Ruben took her hand. "How are you? You look … you look …"

"Focus, Ruben, you know the word you want to say."

Ruben sadly smiled. "Sick."

She took a deep breath, looked around and lowered her voice. "Can I tell you a secret?"

"Sure."

"I got hurt, Ruben. When we were hit by the wave, I got hurt. I don't know how exactly. I'm in pain, I want to cry, I'm weak, dizzy, and I think … no, I know I'm dying."

"Mindy. No. No. Maybe you're hungry, or dehydrated. I am sure you're fine."

"I'm not a medical professional, but I know this isn't fine." She lifted her sweatshirt exposing her swollen stomach. Her belly button was dark and a purple ring formed around it. She touch her skin. "Hard as a rock and it isn't those abs I have been trying to get back."

"Mindy, we will get you help. I will get you help."

Emotional, Mindy spoke with a whimper. "Isn't it too late?"

"No. It is never too late." Ruben placed his arm around her, drawing her nearer to him.

She just wanted to fold, crumble right there, then she heard CJ's voice and she sat up, wiping her eyes.

"You alright?" CJ asked as he approached.

"Yes, fine. I missed Ruben."

"I bet. And I bet you're glad he's fine. I got you a water." He extended a bottle to her. "One of those expensive, fancy ones. I figured since you were a celebrity, this is what you drank."

"Thank you." Mindy reached for it.

"Hey Ruben," Abby called then appeared from the escalator. "Your radio is picking up. We have the Emergency Alert giving instructions." Just as fast as she appeared she raced away.

"I need to hear this," CJ said.

"Me, too," said Mindy.

"You need help?" Ruben asked her.

"I'm fine. I'm fine," Mindy stood. While she still felt horrible, internally she was happy. The emergency alert was good news. Help was out there, somewhere. All was not lost.

They gathered around in silence listening to the yellow radio that Ruben had to wind twice during the long message.

This message will repeat.

Due to multiple volcanic eruptions, the following areas are under immediate evacuation ...

Then the computerized voice went on to list states.

Evacuation stations are located in cities that are designated by states. Please visit your state's stations only. Space at refugee camps is limited to first come basis.

For safety purposes, extreme caution should be exercised when in the vicinity of the greater Phoenix area, if at all possible, it is advised to avoid that area.

Use caution when traveling.

Use caution when traveling outdoors. Volcanic ash is dangerous to the respiratory system.

The announcement was seven minutes long by the time all dangers were listed and evacuation stations announced.

Guy was ready, he waited for the cities to be named for those leaving southern California. Paper and pen in hand he prepared to write down the locations, but didn't need to. There were only three for those in California.

Tucson, Las Cruces, and Midland.

Wouldn't every major area, even small town, still standing, still functioning, be open to helping and aiding those seeking refuge?

It was the largest exodus in history, how were they to fit in such minimal places?

Guy believed there was one of two reasons for that. Either there wasn't that many people left to exodus or there weren't that many places left to go.

In any event, they couldn't wait.

They had to hit the road soon before they wouldn't be able to leave at all.

TWENTY-SIX

Selma, Alabama

The arm sleeve edges of the thick, knit, red cardigan sweater were tattered and torn and it wasn't from age or use. She had found the sweater, poking out of the rubble when the clothes on her back were soaking wet. Cold, tired and sad, she grabbed hold of it, and hadn't taken it off in three days.

Of course, she hadn't stopped moving for three days either. For three days she coasted by on pure luck and emotion, not skill.

There was no reason she should have been alive, but she was. The day it started her mind was preoccupied. She teetered between making idle conversation before the presentation and checking her phone. She sipped coffee from a fine china cup, staring at her phone, finding privacy against the back wall, on the top floor meeting room of a fifteen story building in Washington, D.C...

Her husband was there as well, she worked for his firm. He was by the windows, subtly trying to get her attention.

She would signal to him with a raised index finger. He smiled, but she knew he was frustrated.

That was where she was when the object soared from the sky. Its connection with the atmosphere creating such a sonic boom, the ground vibrated and every window shattered.

Everyone was shocked when it happened and panic ensured on that floor when the sky on the eastern horizon seemed to light up with fire.

Was it a bomb? No one knew.

A hundred people in that room, some bloodied from glass, raced toward the only exit, a single set of heavy oak double doors.

The more people raced to get out, the farther from the doors she was pushed.

"You have to go," her husband told her. "Get downstairs."

"What about you?"

"I'll be there. Go."

But she didn't want to. There were far too many people rushing forward. She feared being trampled and deliberately waited behind.

People shoved and pushed when an orderly exit would have moved much faster. It was in the middle of the chaos, when someone shouted, 'Jesus, there's nowhere to run."

Her curiosity caused her to look for the voice, and she saw a man, his name she didn't know, staring out the window.

"Oh my God," her husband gasped out.

Then she saw it. It moved toward them. A wall of water, crushing everything in its path, taking out buildings as it crashed her way. It was loud and roaring.

She hurriedly backed up, but quickly realized, like the man shouted, there was nowhere to run. For years she hadn't believed in God, but that moment, she subscribed to the aphorism 'there are no atheists in foxholes' and dropped to her knees, praying the end would be painless.

The arriving wave was the backdrop behind her husband as he reached out his hand to her. She merely called out his name, "James." When the wave arrived.

She was so stifled with fear, she didn't breathe, and was already holding her breath when the water pushed through the broken windows.

The last thing she saw was something in the water hit into James. It hit him with such a force, a red cloud of blood erupted around him as his lifeless body 'whooshed' by her.

She was moved by the water, but it forced her against a wall and one of those heavy oak doors, pinned her there.

She was trapped.

There was no way to swim or move. The water engulfed her. She held her breath as long as she could, feeling the water fill her ears and the pressure of the door as it hit against her chest. She looked around for a way to escape, but there was none. She was in a water world.

Just as she was unable to hold her breath any longer, was ready to let go and give into what was always described as a peaceful death, the pressure of the water against the door ceased. Within moments, the water level lowered. Not much but at least to her chest and she gasped out for air, then coughed. Arching her head back, she saw the sky. The roof of the building had been completely removed.

Still semi pinned, she pushed the door away from her. It wasn't on its hinges. It slammed down to the water then flipped up violently. She jumped out of the way in a nick of time.

But the current was still strong, it started to carry her away. Panicked, she grabbed on to whatever she could and that was the oak door that floated freely.

Grasping to the edges of it, she looked around, the entire wall where the windows were, was gone. All she saw was water.

"Anyone!" she yelled out. "Anyone else alive?"

No one answered.

It took all of her strength to lift her body up onto the flat surface of that door. And like Rose from the Titanic, she used the door as her own floatation device.

As the water slightly and slowly receded it drew her out and she saw the remains of the city.

The dome of the Capital was like an island, emerging from the water with little damage, while the Washington Monument looked like skeletal remains of a building.

She floated for a long time, laying flat on that door. She through of her husband and tried to register how he was gone. She thought of how she didn't want to die. More than anything, she thought about her son. Did he know what happened in Washington, Did he fear his mother was dead? She needed to talk to him, tell him she was fine. It was out there in the water, she saw she was one of many people who miraculously survived that wave and now floated on anything they could find.

It wasn't until the sky began to darken that a boat rescued her. She was cold and shivering. There were others on board the motor boat, no one spoke. She watched as they moved farther from D.C.. How far had the waters come in?

Far enough that she was still on the water come nightfall when she was transferred to another boat. This one bigger, like a ferry, It was jammed with people. They had a canteen with weak coffee. But it was hot. She shivered uncontrollably, listening to people talking, trying to figure out what had happened.

On that ferry she learned it was as close to the end of the world as it could get.

The wave, the meteor, wasn't just exclusive to Washington, it was the entire country, the world. Even worse for her, she heard that the entire western seaboard, not only was hit, but devastated by a series of earthquakes. Tsunamis were imminent.

It was after daylight that the ferry made it to dry land. She expected guidance, help, maybe even a government aid station, but nothing was there.

Only rubble. She didn't even know where she was.

No one said anything. No one pointed her in the right direction. There were no answers. They were told to disembark, the ferry pulled away and she along with other were left in destruction.

That's when she spotted the red sweater. It was the one and only thing that kept her warm. Happy that she was on dry land, and believing she saw the last of water, she began a journey on foot and moved like a nomad in a large group of people. She was fortunate when a dump truck pulled up and randomly gave five people a ride. She was one of them.

When that dump truck reached its destination, fate handed her another ride with a family going southwest, returning from a beach vacation.

Cramped in a fetal position she rode in the hatch portion of their SUV. Their home was flattened by an earthquake when they arrived. She slept for a few hours in the back of their vehicle before leaving on foot. Still not knowing where she was.

Her hopes of never seeing flooded land again were washed away, when wet pavement turned into a thin layer of water. She trudged on. Her body was tired, achy, her stomach cramped with hunger pains and she realized her last drink of anything was twenty four hours earlier on that ferry.

There was no dry land. Not as far as the eye could see. She was surrounded by water. It went from her ankles to her knees and by the time it reached her thighs, she had to stop.

She spotted a car poking out of the water and made her way to that, climbing on top of the roof, to get out of the water. Sitting there, she brought her knees to her chest, cradling her arms around her legs. The feeling of desperation and isolation was overwhelming.

But fate would be on her side again. It wasn't long after she heard the sound of a motor. As it grew louder, she saw in the distance a small boat.

She stood up, waving her arms and shouting. She thought for sure the boat didn't see her, but he changed direction and headed her way.

Exasperated and exhausted she sobbed out in gratefulness when the older man in the boat pulled up to her. He cut the motor on the boat as he pulled up to the car.

"Get in," he said with a deep southern accent. "You okay?"

"Yes. Yes, thank you. Thank you so much."

He held out this hand to her, aiding her inside. "Watch your step. There's a blanket back there. You look cold."

"I am. Thank you." She stepped into the small motorized fishing boat. A blanket was tossed on a cooler and she grabbed it. "Oh my God, thank you so much. Are you a rescue boat?"

"No, ma'am, I am just a guy trying to find a way out of this water. You don't sound like you're from around here," he said.

"I'm not. I just took ride after ride. I don't even know where here is."

"Selma," he said.

"Alabama?" she asked. "At least I'm in the right direction."

"Where were you headed?"

"West," she replied.

"So am I. Gonna start the motor again, don't know how long gas will last. We may drift a spell."

"That's fine. I'm grateful."

"Well, I'm Tom." He nodded.

She smiled. "Kylie," she said. "My name is Kylie."

"Nice to meet you. What's out west?"

"My son. He's six. He is with his father. I don't know how, but I have to find him. I have to find my son."

"I hope you do," Tom said, then he started the motor on the boat.

TWENTY-SEVEN

"It's gonna get worse before it gets better," the driver, an air force Sergeant, told Charles right after they left Cheyenne.

He was right.

They moved at a good pace at first, then it began to slow down as the thick heavy ash coated the roads.

Charles was reminded of his youth in New England. The treacherous roads blanketed in snow. Moving slowly so as not to slide. Only with the snow, they didn't have to pull over every hour or so.

Sergeant Lawson was informed. He had been part of a rescue and recovery aid group years earlier for a volcanic eruption in Iceland. He learned a few tricks. One of which was the leaf blower. Before the exhaust, engine and filtering system could become irreversibly clogged. He pulled over, cracked that gas powered blower and cleared out the ash before moving on.

But the farther they traveled the ash was worse. Charles could only imagine how bad it was where they had just left.

He knew they only had an hour or so left before they had to stop for the night. There was no way they'd see in the complete dark with the falling ash. He didn't even want to think about the morning, and hoped they weren't buried while waiting for a little bit of daylight.

He had dosed off just a short span when he felt the truck stop. He thought it was another 'blow and clear' moment, but realized it wasn't, when he heard the voices outside the truck. He couldn't make out what they were saying. They were muffled and sounded as if they were shouting.

Charles slipped into his rain coat, placed on his face mask, secured his boots, and after lifting his hood, stepped from the truck.

He couldn't tell from looking out the window, but as soon as he stepped out he saw they were in a small town.

The ash came to his mid-calf, and the buildings of the town

were barely seen through the falling ash. In fact, everything was barely seen. He spotted Lawson and another soldier standing a few feet ahead of the truck. When he walked to them, he saw why they had stopped.

The entire road was blocked with cars. They were lined up, some had the doors open.

"Sergeant?" Charles called him.

Lawson shouted over the wind and thunder noise. "This is the route that would take us to I-10. Appears some sort of exodus was happening here. Higgins went up about two blocks. It's cars and trucks as far as we can see."

"What do we do?" Charles asked.

"We'll have to back track, sir," Lawson said. "It'll add another two hours to our journey and the alternate route will bring us in just east of Phoenix. It's an hour of backtracking."

"An hour of backtracking?" Charles asked. "Should we just stop here for the night?"

Lawson shook his head. "No, sir, I believe we need to be on our route to stop."

Charles nodded. "I see cars, I see a town. Where are the people? Were they evacuated from here?"

"No, sir, they're here." Lawson took a step and swiped his hand over the driver's side window of a car.

The single cleared area exposed a man in the driver's seat. His head back, mouth open.

"What …?" Charles, startled moved to his right.

"Watch your step."

Charles stopped and looked down.

He felt horrified when he saw and instinctively wanted to run. At first, he didn't notice, but as soon as he was made aware he saw them around the cars, on the ground, ash covered mounds that could only be the bodies of those of the town.

"My God, what happened here? How?" Charles asked.

"Something held up the exit route," Lawson said. "Traffic came to a halt, the ash fell. They suffocated."

"All of them?"

"As far as we can see. And it wasn't fast, it was slow, judging by the looks of them."

"How did this happen to all of them?"

"I'm not a scientist, but I know, if an area is dense like this, and the cloud dense, it creates like seal, almost like a carbon monoxide effect."

"An air inversion?"

"Exactly."

"And we're in the middle of it?" Charles asked.

"Pretty much so, yeah."

"I'll meet you back there." Without saying any more, Charles back tracked quickly to the truck.

The radio call was like chatting with an old friend. It lacked the protocol of 'Roger that' and 'Over', but Charles was more than a colleague to Parker, he *was* an old friend.

Charles described the scene to him that they came across in that small town. Immediately, Parker's knowledge of lesser known history popped in his mind. Being from Pennsylvania, Parker was well aware of the story of the Donora Smog. A small town in southern Pennsylvania, where the pollution for the steel mills was so bad, it trapped a noxious fog close to the ground, killing dozens of people and sickening seven thousand.

When he heard Charles encountered similar, he thought of Donora.

"No one is out here," Charles told him. "No one. We haven't seen a vehicle or a person walking."

"Where are they?"

"I don't know. They either got a jump or they're digging in. It's destitute out here."

"Are you staying safe?"

"To be honest, I'm a little worried about what I saw in that small town. It hit them, it could hit us."

"It's also possible," Parker said. "That ash cut off oxygen and trapped the Carbon monoxide from the running cars. You said there were a lot."

"There were."

"Where are you now?"

"I haven't a clue. We stopped for the night. We had to. It's so damned black we could drive off a cliff and not see it coming with the headlights reflecting off the ash."

"Sounds scary."

"It is," Charles said. "What about you? How are things there?"

"Good. We're staying ahead of it." Parker told him, but that wasn't really the truth. He brushed over any questions about Cheyenne, focusing more on Charles' pilgrimage. He didn't want his friend to worry, and there was good cause.

The ash was so heavy, it already started blocking the vents. Despite the extensive ventilation system in the mountain, the ash was making its way through, and with limited power, there was no way to keep it out.

It was valiant effort, but Parker knew it was a matter of days before he and the hundreds remaining would have to reply on the tainted outside air by making camp close to the tunnel entrances. After a few more minutes of talk, Parker bid goodnight and a safe trip to Charles. He asked him to check in and keep him posted even though he feared prospect of a better world beyond the ash and destruction was slim.

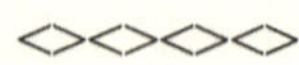

It had to be the thirtieth time CJ listened to the recorded announcement. A part of him hoping that at some point it would change. The non-emotional, robotic voice just made everything sound so final.

They had stopped for the night, unable to move forward in the dark. It wasn't an easy journey, and tarps from the toy company served as ash filters. Not very well. CJ could feel and hear the occasional sputter of the engine.

He didn't drive. He rode in the back of the big truck with Carter and Mindy. Others took turns riding shotgun in the two vehicles. Ruben drove the truck and his father was the driver of the tanker. That was until they stopped, then Guy joined the others in the back of the truck to get some rest.

CJ didn't want to leave the tanker, even if it meant sleeping in there. A tanker with gas was a valuable asset. Even though they hadn't seen another vehicle, he didn't want to take a chance of it getting stolen. That was of course, if anyone could see it.

When he switched spots with his father, CJ couldn't see his hand in front of his face. Mindy wanted to join him and keep him company, she huddled close to him using his as her guide. The flashlight did very little to illuminate anything. It did, however, give some light to the cab of the fuel truck, so CJ and Mindy weren't in complete darkness.

His mind wandered a lot sitting out there. Starting the truck every once and a while to listen to the radio. Mindy wasn't much company, she fell asleep shortly after getting in the fuel truck.

They talked about Rose and Marty, envisioning them as a young couple, what they could have been like.

CJ wished he would have asked them more about their lives, their families, he didn't. He left bad about that.

The disaster was rough on him physically and every time he stopped, his body felt it. Emotionally, since he found Carter, CJ was okay. He didn't think about the world that was gone, he thought about the world he had to live in.

Finally, he fell asleep. The first restful sleep he had in days. Seat reclined back, head tilted to his left, he slept dreamless and hard until a bright light and blast of cold hair stirred him away.

He jolted, fearful something was wrong. The light was the interior light of the cab and the air came from the passenger door that had not closed all the way.

She obviously slipped out in a rush. He grabbed his flashlight, wanting to find her. He thought maybe she had to go really bad until he heard what sounded like choking.

Hurriedly, he crawled across to the passenger door, turned on the flashlight, ready to use it as a guide when he stepped out. When he pushed up the passenger's door, He saw Mindy. Lit some by the interior light, she was standing, hunched over, her back to him. With coughing and choking sounds her back moved up and down.

"Mindy?" He called her.

"Oh, God, CJ, I feel so sick."

"Are you throwing up?" he asked.

She slowly turned around, nodding. When she did he lifted the beam of the flashlight to her.

Mindy brought the back of her hand across her mouth and then lowered it, exposing what looked like blood on her mouth and chin.

"Jesus, Mindy." CJ jumped out of the fuel truck.

"What? What is it?"

His landing feet caused a huge cloud of ash and he raced the few feet to her

"I'm okay now, it didn't feel like much."

CJ shone the light. Her regurgitation formed a small indentation in the deep ash. CJ wanted to cry when he saw it. It wasn't that Mindy had vomited, it was the fact that Mindy had vomited blood.

TWENTY-EIGHT

More than anything CJ wanted to leave immediately, but he knew that wasn't possible. He felt helpless and wanted to do something for Mindy. She couldn't even hold down water.

When she seemed to finally fall asleep, CJ slipped from the fuel truck and hurried to the tractor trailer where he woke Ruben.

"She's bad. Really bad Ruben."

Perhaps that wasn't the best way to wake him up, but he snapped to attention.

"What's going on?" Ruben asked.

"She's throwing up blood."

"Oh my God." Ruben immediately jumped from the truck.

"I want to leave as soon as humanly possible," CJ said.

"Absolutely."

They had driven to that point at a snail's pace. Had it been before the events, they would have already been in Tucson, but a simple six hour trip was complicated by the hard falling ash and the fact they were told to avoid Phoenix.

Finally, they caught a break. The sky lightened enough for them to roll out. The ash was bad, deep and slippery, but they had hit the plateau with it. Soon, the ash lessened the farther south they went. And while the skies continued to be gray and dismal, it wasn't as dark and ominous. The lightning and falling ash were replaced with severe winds and pounding rain.

They were moving. The roads seemed like they were cleared for an exodus, when it fact it was just barren. No one traveled the road, almost as if no one was left. They were still rolling through earthquake land. That was evident by the toppled roadside buildings and buckling of the highway.

They stopped twice before Tucson. Once for a bathroom break and the second at a roadblock fifteen miles from the refugee relief station.

"Where are you headed?" the soldier at the roadblock asked CJ.

"We're headed to the refugee relief station."

"Well, you'll have to turn around, back track six miles and hit I-10 again, head east to Las Cruces."

"Why?"

"The Tucson RRS is closed."

"Closed? How can that be?"

"It's to capacity. Not taking any more. Seems a lot of folks fleeing Phoenix arrived. Sorry."

At that moment CJ could have pleaded for Mindy's life. He could have. He didn't. He opted for lying.

"Well, we're not staying," CJ said. "This is a fuel tank. We're dropping it off and that truck has supplies."

The fuel truck was easy to get away with. A tractor trailer with supplies... not so much. CJ's heart pounded, expecting the soldier to inspect the truck. Instead, he let them through. Probably because he didn't want to be out in the hard rain any longer than he had to.

The refugee camp was set up south of Tucson and with the flat terrain, CJ could see how massive it was. The amount of cars left on the side of the road, also told him that.

Just after the sign that stated 'no vehicles beyond this point', CJ stopped the fuel truck on the already crowded road. He walked alone to the soldier post.

"I don't know how you got through or why they let you through," the soldier said. "We aren't taking anyone. As much as we'd like to we are beyond capacity."

"What are we supposed to do?" CJ asked with desperation. "I have a very sick woman. She was injured and it's bad."

"How bad?"

"It's internal bleeding."

The soldier looked back at the tractor. "Listen I can let her through and one of you to help. The rest have to stay..."

"Thank you, thank you so much."

"But I want to show you something." He inched CJ up the road and pointed. "See that man in the red jacket?"

CJ looked. He did see a man with a red jacket, standing close to the entrance area of the camp. "Yes. What about him."

"He's the end of the line. That line wraps all the way back and around. That's the line to see the two doctors we have here. The wait is over four hours."

"But she has life threatening injuries."

"Many of those people can't even walk."

"Oh my god."

"I do have a suggestion. You can wait in that line or … unlike others that walked, you have an option."

CJ gave the soldier his attention.

Ruben had climbed into the refueler to keep Mindy company.

"Oh, this is cozy," he said. "Roomy too. Not as roomy as the one I drove for my license. Mindy's head tilted to the left and she lifted her eyes at Ruben.

"We'll get you better." He grabbed her hand.

The door to the fuel truck can opened and it was Guy. "How you hanging in there, kid?'

"I'm hanging in there."

"Good. Because it looks like my son is making progress. He's coming back now."

"Where's Carter?" Mindy asked.

"He's in the other truck. He's fine."

CJ approached. "Hey."

"Hey," Ruben said. "What's going on?"

"We have a choice. We can stay, they'll let Mindy in but there is a four hour wait to see a doctor."

"Four hours?" Guy barked. "We can be in Las Cruces by then."

Ruben added. "And risk waiting another four hours."

"Or …" CJ said. "The soldier said we could head to Mexico. We can be in Nogales in an hour. They opened the border."

"I don't think we have a choice here," said Guy. "We go to Mexico."

"No," Mindy said weakly. "No we don't. You don't CJ, you can't leave the country. You can't take Carter to Mexico. What if she's looking for him?"

"Who?" Guy asked.

"Carter's mom," Mindy answered. "She's his mother. She loved him. What if she's out there searching? She'll never find him. Ever..."

"Mindy." CJ said. "You need help. I can come back."

"What if you can't?" she asked. "No. I'm dying, CJ, I know it. I'm dying. Please. Let's just go to Las Cruces."

CJ lowered his head.

"I can take you to Mexico," Guy said. "I'll drive you and anyone else that wants to go."

Mindy whimpered. "Then another child is without a parent."

"What about me?" Ruben asked. "I can take you to Mexico."

Mindy shook her head. "You are headed to Texas to find your son. You can't stop that mission."

"Well," Guy sighed out. "We're headed to Las Cruces, then. But … Mexico is on the table. It wasn't when we took off. We should give the others the option. It's closer, it's refuge."

"How are we going to do that?" CJ asked. "We have twenty-one people."

"We'll steal a car if we have to," Guy said. "Plenty left on the road. I'll go speak to the others."

After Guy had left, CJ reached cross Ruben for Mindy. "You are dying. Please don't give up. Not yet."

Mindy fought the tears, she didn't reply, she just grasped tightly to CJ's hand.

The boat drifted now. The gas for the motor long since ran out and it was a matter of going where the current led.

There was no end in sight.

Kylie learned a lot about the man that rescued her from the roof top. Other than his name was Tom, he was seventy-four years old, a retired mechanic, that never did 'get' the newfangled cars. He liked to fish and did that a lot, and he was traveling from his home in West Virginia to find his wife, daughter and granddaughter who were taking a tri-generation gambling junket to Vegas.

He could have gone straight west, through Ohio and Indiana, but he was a man who listened to word of mouth. That 'I heard this and that' informed him that middle America was struck.

He figured south.

He hadn't heard of the water problem, and didn't know how and when the flooding started.

Both of them had figured it was more than flooding. The water area was too vast.

As much as he was a knowledgeable fisherman, boating man, dedicated husband and father, Tom was a movie trivia guru.

"How long have we been drifting?" Kyle asked.

Tom looked at his watch. "Going on six hours."

"How far do you think we went?"

"Not far. Now you don't worry about that. We'll get somewhere soon."

"What if it rains?" Kylie asked.

"I got a tarp. It might not be comfortable, we may have to hunch but we won't take in water," said Tom. "Now go on. It's your turn. We can't sit here saying 'are we there yet' we have to keep busy. Go."

"What's the score?'

"Twelve to three. Me."

Kylie exhaled heavily. "Okay. Ready. Water."

"Of course."

"Door."

"Titanic."

"Are you kidding me?" Kylie asked. "All I said door."

"Well, considering we're only doing movies that deal with water and you said door, that was a big clue. Don't give it away so fast."

"I had my own Titanic moment."

"You did?" Tom asked. "When?"

"In D.C. The wave hit. I still don't know how I survived. But I floated on a door."

"Could you fit another person on that door?"

Kylie laughed. "I always thought that about that movie."

"Yeah, me, too. Then I heard the theory that Jack was in her imagination."

"I never heard that."

"You're stalling," Tom said. "Afraid of mine."

"Go on."

"Dry land is not a myth, I've seen it."

"I have too," Kyle said.

"No, it's a hint a movie. Kevin Costner." He watched he shake her head. "Gills? No. Waterworld. The movie."

"Never heard of it or Kevin whatever."

"Wow. I'm old."

"Tom," Kylie said gently. "Thank you. I mean it. I would be a mess right now if it wasn't for you. Your family is very lucky to have you."

"It goes both ways kid." He winked. "Now. Your turn."

Kylie wasn't as fast as Tom, she had to take some time to think about a movie. Thinking kept her mind occupied and she needed that instead of dwelling on the nearly impossible task she had a head of her.

Cheyenne Mountain, Colorado

The ash ended up being the least of the concerns, volunteer crews were dispatched every few hours to clear the heavy stuff and then through the quick thinking and mechanical skills of one of the survivors, they were able to use the technology from the blast valves by the doors to clear the ash that made its way into the ventilation system.

Even Parker wasn't aware of the blast valves. He was certain the colonel didn't know either. It took a survival enthusiast to tell them about it, when plans were made to move people to the East slope tunnel entrance. It was an ingenious update done in the eighties. A way to keep contaminated air out of the bunker by blasting outward for twenty seconds.

The bunker was operational.

There was enough water to last months, and the natural spring ensured it wouldn't run out. Food wasn't as plentiful, but with the proper rationing, they could spread it out.

In its heyday over six hundred people worked at Cheyenne Mountain. There were sleeping facilities for hundreds of people.

Instead of diverting attention to squeezing everyone into tunnels, Parker worked with the Colonel to get those who stayed behind situated.

It was an almost party atmosphere.

Once Parker saw Colonel Rush's men were initiating things, he made his way back to the communication room to wait to hear from Charles. It had been since the night before, over fourteen hours and nothing. It wasn't a communication breakdown either. They were in contact with Tucson. That camp was full and taking names. Registering them.

Charles should have been at his destination.

He feared the worst. Charles was the one to get things started outside, on the ground, where people needed it.

Parker started rethinking the idea of staying behind. He was elected by the people, yet, he wasn't with the people.

He would do his part from inside the bunker. Do what he could. Along with Charles, though it didn't seem possible, they could conceivably come up with a long range plan.

While waiting to hear from him, Parker looked at the satellite images of Earth. A lot of the Eastern Hemisphere was shrouded in a black hovering cloud, one that grew each hour. The Yellowstone Caldera was still active and there was so much debris from the meteors that a haze glassed over the earth like a bad Photoshop filter.

Water was in places it shouldn't be,

The world was a mess.

Parker knew there was no cleaning it up, no quick fix to make it better for those who survived. They only thing they could do was make it livable, anyway, any how, they could.

If he had to make the choice, Guy would have chosen Mexico, as well. To him, there really wasn't a reason not to head south and arrive in a safe location in an hour's time. He couldn't blame anyone who decided to take that route.

In Tucson the group divided. It wasn't a heartbreaking split, after all Guy didn't know any of them. Most of the people that were with CJ were strangers walking together. That was why it came as no surprise when given the option, everyone chose Mexico.

Abby didn't. She decided to go with familiarity. Even though she didn't know them long, she knew Guy, Ruben and Carter.

The cab of the small capacity fuel truck wasn't large. Two comfortable size front bucket seats and a rest bed directly behind them. The six of them crammed in there for the journey. CJ drove, Guy shared a seat with Carter, Abby sat on the floor, while Mindy and Ruben sat on the rest bed.

Mindy wasn't well. Guy wasn't a doctor, but common sense told him she was failing fast. Even though he was aware from talking to Ruben that Mindy previously had a substance abuse problem, he believed it was too late to worry about it and offered her some of his jackpot he lifted from TSA. Mindy finally opted for the cannabis drops. They helped some, relaxing and relieving her pain a little.

Guy just hoped that got somewhere soon. The last thing he wanted for Mindy was to have her final moments crammed in the cab of a small field truck.

Very little ash fell in the part of the country where they drove. It was such a fine amount, that CJ couldn't tell at times if it was ash or dust from the desert like area.

It didn't need destruction, earthquakes, meteors or volcanos, to CJ, the route they drove was desolate. Like something out of a horror film where a family takes a road trip and gets stranded in the middle of nowhere.

They passed two roadside shops and gas stations, both were closed and obviously ransacked, taken for everything that had.

He wasn't familiar with the area but he was certain there had to be more towns and places where they possibly could get some help.

CJ wasn't aware at first of the 'every town for itself' mentality that swept the nation in the wake of global disaster. The reality hit him in a big way.

Whoever coined the idiom 'All roads lead to Rome' surely had no idea a thousand years later that phrase would fit a small New Mexico town with a population under three thousand.

He quickly learned that all roads headed east across New Mexico had to go through Lordsburg, or at least it seemed that way.

CJ couldn't see anything that even remotely resembled a town, but a sign prior indicated it was ahead. He did see the turn off for the rest area, which was blocked off.

In fact, everything was blocked off. It appeared to be they were building something. A fence perhaps or wall? It was still in the early stages and CJ couldn't tell.

Both side of the highway were closed with a horizontally parked vehicles just before the turn for the rest area.

He could see the people on the other side of the highway, they faced west in case someone tried to take that way.

There was a sheriff's car ahead of CJ. Three men and a woman, all holding weapons stood on the road wearing bandanas over their mouths like some sort of bandits.

"What the hell is this?" Guy asked, then pulled out the map. "They're blocked the way through."

"Maybe they're just checking vehicles as pass into town," CJ said.

"Maybe."

"I'll pull a little closer."

"Listen," Abby said. "Show your hands right away. If they won't let you through, barter. Find their sweet spot. Everyone has a price.

Guy looked at her. "I'm gonna take it this advice isn't from some psychology class you took."

"No. No, I was preparing for a role. I was playing a waitress in a siege and I researched."

"Yes, thank you," Guy said. "CJ just inch up."

CJ did. He parked about fifty feet from the barricade. He informed the others he'd be back and he and Guy stepped out at the same time.

"Hold it right there," the officer said.

CJ raised his hands. "We aren't armed." He turned around slowly. "See? We aren't armed."

"Well, that's all kinds of stupid considering what's happening," the officer said.

"Can we come closer so we don't have to shout?" CJ asked.

"You can come closer, you're not getting through."

After looking at Guy, CJ walked toward the barricade and when he approached he introduced himself. "My name is Carter James, CJ, this is my father, Guy."

Guy nodded.

CJ eyed the officer's badge. "Listen, Deputy Graham, are you in charge?"

"I'm one of a few in charge. Town's closed son. There's no need to speak to anyone in charge. You can't get through."

"We need to get through," CJ said. "Please. We just need to pass through. We're trying to get to Las Cruces."

"I'm sure you are," Graham said calmly and oddly polite. "Like a lot of others before you. I'm going to tell you the same thing I told them. You cannot pass through our town."

"Why?" Guy asked.

"People are desperate. They lost everything."

"So why not help them?" Guy questioned.

"We can't. Our resources are limited. What we have is what we have. There are no delivery trucks coming. No aid. I have to take care of my own, I am sure you understand that."

"I do," CJ said. "We need to get to Las Cruces."

"And you still can. Just back track fifteen miles, go south on Three-thirty eight until you get to Animas. Head East on Muir then north on One Thirteen. You'll pass through two small areas that aren't going to mind if you pause there. We do. This is only gonna add about an hour or so to your trip."

CJ nodded. "Do they ... do you know if any of them have a doctor."

Graham seemed to find that amusing, he sort of chuckled. "No." he shook his head. "No they don't. Las Cruces does."

"Do you?" Guy asked.

Graham didn't answer, he looked at Guy with almost a pause.

"You do," Guy said.

"Sir, please," CJ pleaded. "Please we have a woman. She was

injured. She needs help. She desperately needs help. Maybe your doctor …"

"I'm sorry," he said. "No."

"Then please let us through. You can escort us through. She's already fighting for her life, please don't make her fight another hour."

Graham shook his head. "Sorry. Just go the other way."

"What if we barter?" CJ asked. "You said you're on limited resources, right? We don't have much food or supplies, I'll be honest there. But we have that." He pointed to the truck. "It's an eight thousand gallon tank and it's almost full. You can check. Check the gauge. You let our woman see your doctor and it's yours. All of it. Take it. If you don't use it you can barter it later. You can't beat that."

"I can help with whatever you're building over there," Guy said. "That's what I did. Plus … I have pot."

"Dad!" CJ scolded.

"Abby said, find a sweet spot. I'm finding a sweet spot"

"To a cop?" CJ asked.

Graham looked at Guy. "You really have pot?"

"Yep."

"Dad," CJ warned.

"How much?"

"Lots."

"Dad."

"How do you have lots?" Graham asked.

"We were stranded at the San Bernardino Airport. TSA must have made some sort of bust, plus other stuff they had in a locker. Hit the freaking marijuana jackpot. Vapes, oils …"

"Do you have the actual plant, dry form, seeds?"

"Yeah, some."

CJ shifted his eyes from the cop to his dad. Watching them bounce back and forth, question and answer, wondering when the officer was going to slap the cuffs on his father.

Graham nodded. "Okay, bring her in. Doc is located just a few blocks in."

"Wait. What? Seriously?" CJ asked. "You'll let your doctor see her."

"Yep. We'll move the Ford for you."

"Wow. I offered you fuel and you let us in for pot?"

"Sweet spot," Guy whispered. "Don't push it."

"Oh, don't get me wrong," Graham said. "We're taking your fuel, too. But we need that pot. We have a couple sick people in this town. My wife is one of them. She has MS. I'm thinking ahead." The officer backed up, and hand signaled his people.

CJ was still in disbelief of how it all went down, but it didn't matter. He was happy and relieved. They were going through, and Mindy was going to get the help she needed.

TWENTY-NINE

Charles and the convoy arrived in Midland Texas just before nightfall. It was a moonless sky, blackened with dark clouds, but Charles knew the second they pulled into the city limits that there was a glimmer of hope.

They still had power.

Or at least had it up and running again.

They followed the hand painted signs to the relief area. It was an ambitious endeavor. Although it was partially erected, Charles could see they still had a long way to go and crews were working diligently.

It was set up in the Westridge Park neighborhood of Midland. Specifically in the eight square mile section that where the baseball field, football stadium, sports complex and all surrounded parking areas.

It was going to be huge.

The moment he arrived he was greeted and escorted to what he learned was the headquarters tent. There were tables inside a few cots and a canteen of coffee. He had just helped himself to a cup when the Governor walked in.

"Charles," Governor Brad Wallerman extended his hand. "Good to see you."

"Brad." Charles shook his head and gave him an embrace. "You made it out."

"I wasn't in town when it hit." Brad pursed his lips. "Unfortunately my family was there."

"I am so sorry."

"Me, too. This keeps me busy. I'm focusing. That's all I can do."

"This is quite impressive. How did you do all this so fast?"

"Well, the shit hit the fan so to speak, I had to make choice," Brad said. "I could use all of our resources for search and rescue or

I could divide it. Looking at the circumstances I had to focus on those who survived. This is one of three in the states. We pulled all of our FEMA resources, then we hit and seized the public places. Unfortunately, if need be we will hit the private sectors. Anti-hoarding laws are in effect."

"How many people are here?" Charles asked.

"Close to nine thousand. We have even started the registry yet. We've taken names of about half. It's overwhelming and more are coming in."

"Communications?"

"Sparse. We do our best. Most of this is word of mouth, trucks with bullhorns and what was playing on radios from the feds. Unfortunately, the Emergency Alert system cut out about four hours ago. It's been silent."

"I know you were in contacts with our team when I was north," Charles said. "Anything?"

"Not for a while. Do you think everything is alright up there?"

"I hope."

Brad exhaled. "To be honest, I can't concern myself with that. I have to focus on what I can do as a central hub here. That's my goal. Make this a central hub and headquarters. I can't sit and wait, for things to show up. If I do that … I could be making a grave mistake. So I am not operating on the notion that we, like every other state, is on our own."

Charles heard him and understood. He was there now and ready to do whatever Brad needed, but unlike Brad he wasn't ready to give up on the president. Not yet.

Thigs were underway, an effort to save people. How long that would last, he didn't know. Even though the alert message stopped playing, the word had gotten out. Thousands had arrived and Charles had no reason to believe thousands more would soon follow.

At least he hoped so.

Cheyenne Mountain, Colorado

"Charles, come in. Are you there?" Parker made the radio call again. "Come in."

Nothing.

He had hit the radio every hour on the hour and had no luck. No call saying they had to stop for the night. No word.

Parker had to believe they made it.

"How about on your end?" he asked Colonel Rush.

"Sir, we have nothing. We have lost our final line out. No communications."

"How about outside the United States?"

"We're down."

"How is that possible? I mean hours ago we were up and running."

"The ash hasn't stopped falling," Rush said. "It's still coming down, the volcano is still erupting. The problem is, it will keep erupting. The more it does so, the more ash that comes down on us. The last crew out there reported storms that seemed like something from a sci fi movie. Geographically we are not in a good position and this bunker wasn't designed with a massive volcanic eruption in mind."

"Could we be buried or struck in here."

"No, there are many ways out of this bunker. Getting out of here is not the problem, leaving the area is a whole different story."

Parker was a man on very little sleep and with a lot on his mind. He had been in the communications room for hours and needed a break. He decided to take a walk and that walk led him to the southwest slop entrance.

There were soldiers and other personnel in that tunnel, and looked like they had made a home there. Tents and tables set up, cots and sleeping bags.

He immediately felt a difference in that tunnel. The temperature was colder, there was a slight smell of sulfur and it was loud. He could hear incredibly strong thunder clashes that sent a vibration through him.

That was when he noticed the blast door was open.

He wanted to ask about it, but he didn't. He kept walking to the door. No one camped by it and only a small amount of ash had blown in. That made sense considering beyond the blast doors were another quarter mile of tunnel until the outside.

As he walked by, people only looked at him. He felt the sense that at some point he stopped being the president.

Really, he wasn't anymore. He was useless. At least he felt that way. He imagined presidents before him would feel similar under the same circumstance. Except maybe Ronald Reagan. Parker always imagined that Reagan had a slight infatuation with the end of the world. If the meteors came during his administration, Reagan would be calm. "Well, Nancy, we're headed to the bunker."

But then, Reagan would have left to govern where he was needed … outside. He wouldn't send his right hand man.

What president would?

It was ironic, that as he slipped through the blast doors he walked into a dark tunnel lit only by dim emergency lights. He was a metaphor in his journey … a man walking down a dark path.

The hollowness of the tunnel amplified the storm. It beat against his ears. He could feel the ash under his feet, it caused his shoes to slide like the stuff on the dance floor.

He followed the bright light at the end of the tunnel, the exterior spotlights were on. They flickered, but it wasn't from lack of power, it was from the ash and rain falling in front of them.

Each step down that tunnel was different. It went from dry to a wet slippery. The rain caused a mist against him. Just as he neared the end, he noticed a sluggish feeling in his walk. He looked down, it was hard to see and he grabbed the small flashlight from his back pocket. His shoes were emerged in a black, thick substance.

He trudged on, only a few more steps and stopped a few feet shy of the opening when he felt the liquid reach his ankles. It moved in a slow flowing manner from the entrance.

It was like tar, thick and black. He swiped his hand down his face, then shone the light on his palm. It was black. Raising his head, he took a closer look at the exterior spotlights. It wasn't just rain falling, it was the same thick black stuff.

Ash had mixed with water creating like a mud and the stuff rained down from the sky.

Parker realized if it looked like that in the tunnel, he didn't want to think about what it looked like outside.

It was done.

As long as the volcano kept erupting, the landscape around the mountain would evolve.

He and the others in the bunker weren't going nowhere. At least for a while. If they could go anywhere at all.

When CJ heard it was a town doctor, he envisioned some man, well past his prime and set in his doctoring ways. He didn't expect Doctor Michael Leopold, a physician in his late thirties with boatloads of energy and compassion. When they brought Mindy to him, he didn't exude gloom and doom.

"Let's have a look at you," he said kindly to her.

"We appreciate this," CJ said.

"Not a problem. If you'll have a seat, I'll be right with you when I'm done examining her."

"Thank you."

The doctor's office looked like it was a hardware store or something at one time. It saw on the corner, large widows. A few minutes after they all sat in the waiting room, a young woman in scrubs walked in. She nodded and headed to the back examining room where Mindy was. She came back out and collected CJ, doctor's orders.

"Doctor Mike said you have a nasty wound infection," she said to him. She had to be in her early twenties, probably fresh out of school. Even her scrubs were newer.

"I do?"

"Yep, you do, gonna clean that up and get you some antibiotics."

"Thank you. How's Mindy?"

"Doctor Mike is tending to her."

After he was finished he went back out in the waiting room. Ruben looked beside himself, genuinely concerned. It was more than an employee to an employer.

"I think he's in love with her," CJ whispered to his father.

"What? Who are you talking about?"

CJ nodded at Ruben.

"Don't be absurd. It's a parental thing. What does it matter anyhow?"

He was about to say, 'it doesn't', when Doctor Mike walked in the waiting room.

They all stood. Except for Carter who was fast asleep.

Doctor Mike looked at the faces. "It's not good."

Abby said, "She ruptured her spleen didn't she?"

Guy looked at her.

"Yes, she did," Doctor Mike replied. "I did an ultrasound, that was all I had to do. It's bad. To be honest with you, I don't know how she is alive. Her entire abdomen is filled with blood, it's pressing on her internal organs. Her heart and lungs are barely functioning and, I spotted clots."

"Can you operate?" Guy asked.

Doctor Mike shook his head. "I can't. I mean … if she were stronger, I'd give it a try. Opening her means putting her under and she won't know her final moments. That, sadly, is where she is."

CJ saw it. Ruben stumbled back some in shock. Guy lowered his head.

"I've given her some morphine to make her comfortable. Like I said, I don't know how she made it this long. She should have passed away from this within twelve hours of the injury. She told me there was no medical help then."

"And she kept walking." CJ said.

"She knew," Doctor Mike said. "And she knows now. I was honest with her. You can go back and see her if you want. I know she'd like that."

CJ nodded.

"I'm sorry. I really am. I wish I could tell you something better," Doctor Mike said.

A part of CJ knew he wasn't going to get good news. Mindy increasingly went downhill, her face grew paler. He was hoping for a miracle but was realistic in knowing there were none.

Guy didn't spend time with her, and Abby didn't know her, so they stayed back while CJ and Ruben made their way to Mindy.

She was wearing oxygen tubing, her face was clean and hair pulled back from her face. Doctor Mike's assistant had cleaned her up. When he really looked at her laying on that table, the back propped, he saw how swollen she really was. His heart sunk.

"Hey," CJ said as he walked closer.

"Hey," she replied

"I know it's stupid to ask, how are you?"

"I'm good. Well, not good. But emotionally, I'm okay with this. It's you two that have to stay back in this world."

"Mindy." CJ lowered his head. "I am sorry this is happening to you. I wish with all my heart you didn't have to go through this."

"But I do. I do. And thank you."

"For what?"

"For taking me on this journey. I need to tell you something," she said weakly. "I never told anyone. Come closer, Ruben, so you can hear." She waited until they were close. "I lied."

"What?" CJ asked.

"I told you stuff. I said my mother was a proud woman. I didn't know if she was."

"What do you mean?" asked CJ.

"Mindy," Ruben said. "You don't need to tell us this."

"I do. I do. We lived on the streets for a long time. My mom tried to take care of me, but the system took me away from her. I remember crying and crying, reaching out to her. She reached out to me and they took me away. I saw her a couple times after that, but they never returned me to her. I was adopted, given a new last name. I searched, you know, I searched for her. When I got old enough I hired detectives. By the time I found her, she had died. But I learned this, she looked for me. She looked for me, too. I believe Carter's mom is out there looking. Please always look for her, too."

"I'll try." CJ laid his hand on her arm. He wanted to retract it, pull back when he felt how cool she was. It frightened him.

"Thank you," she said.

He leaned down to her. "I'm gonna let Ruben have some time with you. Okay?"

Mindy nodded.

"I'll be back," he whispered and kissed her on the forehead. "Thank you for all that you have done for me."

Mindy's lips quivered and she nodded again, trying not to cry.

CJ gave a look to Ruben and slipped from the room.

"Just you and me," Ruben said.

"Like always. You aren't giving up on Stewart are you?"

"Who me? Nah. Never."

"Good. Promise me you'll keep searching."

"With everything I am, I promise you." He grabbed her hand. "I will not give up. I will never give up."

CJ sat down in the chair next to his father with a heavy exhale.

"How is she?" Guy asked.

CJ shook his head. "She so swollen, Dad. Just … it's bad."

"I'm sorry about your new friend."

"Me, too."

CJ closed his eyes and then he heard it. A hissing with a slight whistle sound. He opened one eye and looked to his father.

Guy had a vapor pen, he held in the steam, and showed the pen to CJ.

"No. I thought you handed it all over."

"Not all." Guy exhaled and then coughed, he coughed again. "I told him I hit the jackpot, just didn't say how much there was in there."

"Oh, my God, dad."

Shaking his head, CJ looked at the door when Graham walked in.

"Sorry to hear about how bad your friend is," Graham said.

"Thank you."

"Listen … we really appreciate the truck and the …" he looked at Guy. "Pot. When you need to rest, there's a Best Western down the street." He handed CJ a key card. "Two-twelve." Then handed one to Abby. "Ma'am, Two-Fourteen. Betty made some sandwiches, they are there." Abby took the key with gratefulness and clutched it in her hand. "Thank you so much."

CJ took his card. "Thank you very much. We'll find a way out of here first thing in the morning."

"Yeah, I want to talk to you about that." Graham rubbed his chin. "We appreciate what you gave us. You said you're from the east?"

"D.C., yes," CJ answered.

"You know ... you know it's gone right?" Graham asked. "The whole East Coast is gone. Where are you headed?"

Guy shrugged. "Maybe find one of those refugee relocation camps. That's all we can do."

"Because you gave us that stuff and you have the boy, you're welcome to stay here," Graham said. "I do need some help the fences. And I can use some bodies on post. Think about it. Again, you're welcome."

"We appreciate it." CJ stood and shook his hand. "Thank you for helping Mindy."

"I wish it were more." He turned around, tipped his hat and walked out.

"Now that's good people," Guy said with a point.

"Surprising huh?" CJ said.

"Ruben," Abby said softly.

Both CJ and Guy turned around.

Ruben sighed out with such sadness, closed his eyes tightly and cleared his throat.

"No," CJ groaned out.

"She's gone," Ruben cleared his throat again. "Mindy is gone."

THIRTY

Kyle and Tom had rationed out the rest of the food and had one half bag of chips remaining and a few sip of water. Even though the rain was off and on, they weren't certain about drinking it. If they got to the point that they had to, they would.

They drifted a long time.

Kylie dozed off last, it wasn't by choice. They were both awoke by the sound of shouting and clanking.

The sky wasn't even partially light yet. Kylie looked up to see another boat, this one larger, the passengers looked as bad as Kylie felt, yet then were enthusiastic about helping the drifting duo.

Kylie and Tom gladly accepted the ride.

The boat was motorized and eventually they made landfall.

Feeling so grateful to see it, Kylie joked with Tom, quoting his movie trivia. "Dry land is not a myth."

"No. Not it's not." He smiled putting his arm around her.

They docked just beyond a National Bank and disembarked on a highway overpass. From here they walk. Kylie's legs were weak and wobbled a lot, it took her a good mile of walking until she felt steady.

From the dry land of the overpass to ankle high water, they trudged on under the lightening sky until a school bus picked them up. From there they drove a few hours. Kylie was unsure how long because that was when she fell asleep.

She woke when the bus stopped in front of a building.

The sign on the building read Coahoma County Assistance Office and they were led into a large waiting room where they filled out papers, then led to an office with a many cubicles. Kylie and Tom took a seat before a desk, there was a pamphlet there for expectant mothers.

"Sorry about the wait," a man with a checkered tie sat down. "I see you are from Washington D.C..."

Kylie nodded. "I am."

"Wow, you're the first person I have heard of that has made it out of there."

"There a few others," she said.

"You, sir, are not too far from home."

"Depends where we are," Tom replied.

"Clarksdale, Mississippi."

Tom whistled. "Well aren't we closer to our destinations."

"And where would that be?" the man asked.

"I'm looking for my wife and daughter," Tom answered.

"I'm looking for my son. He is with his father, they were in California."

The man sat back. "You know both those areas were devastated. Not shattering your hope. But letting you know. There are people coming out of Vegas, but not many are coming from California. Now the good news is there are designated refugee centers for different areas, you can start your search there. The registry should be up and running in a week or so. Should make your search easier. Ideally that registry is supposed to be a database, so you can stop at any city and search. But … worst case, you go town by town."

"Thank you," Tom said. "Do you have a center here we can rest up before we move out?"

"We do. We can give you a place to rest," he said. "I'd take a few days. Recover then we can see what we can do about assisting you in your search."

"You are the country assistance office," Tom joked,

"Funny, huh, last week I was approving food benefits. This week, I'm trying to hand it out. Same job, different circumstances."

"We appreciate the help," Tom said.

"If you give me a few more minutes, I'll get you a place to go. Excuse me." He stood and walked from the office.

"We'll find them." Tom patted Kylie's hand.

"I know." Kylie nodded. The man suggested a few days wait, she didn't want to do that. But she understood his reasoning. Going out there, searching before the names were registered was like searching for a needle in a haystack. At least with the designated cities, they'd have direction, and that was a start.

◇◇◇◇

"Hey, Buddy," Ruben spoke in a morning whisper to Carter.

Carter opened his eyes.

"Give me a hug, I'm leaving."

Carter rubbed his eyes. "Are you going to come back?"

"I will eventually, I promise"

Carter sat up and placed his arms around Ruben.

"Be good, okay?"

"I will."

He rubbed his hand over the boy's already messy hair, then tucked him back in and walked from the motel room.

He pulled the door closed behind him chuckling at the dangling 'do not disturb' sign Guy insisted on putting out.

It didn't seem quite as funny when he spotted the housekeeping cart and a maid pushing it.

"Morning," he said to her.

"Morning," she replied.

Carrying his one and only bag, Ruben made his way down the stairs, where CJ and his father were standing by an old pick-up truck.

"Your chariot awaits," Guy said. "Nice of them to give you one."

"Yeah, it is."

"Any idea where you're going?" CJ asked. "Plan of action?"

"Texas. Find the university. Start there. Graham said College Station was hit but not too bad from what he heard. Earthquakes you know. I'm sure there are refugee places there."

"What if he's looking for you?" CJ said.

"A parent looks for their child," Ruben said, looking at Guy. "The child needs to stay put."

"Unless of course, the child is looking for their child," Guy said. "Whole different ball game."

"Fortunately, that's not the case for me." Ruben stepped to Guy and gave him an embrace. "Take care of yourself. I'll be back."

"I'm sure you will. Are you certain you don't want to take Abby? She offered."

"No. And it's simply because I don't know where I'll go or how I'll do it. She needs to stay here." Ruben looked at CJ. "Take care of your dad and that boy."

"I will." CJ shook his hand and opened the door for him.

Ruben tossed in his bag and slipped in.

"Any problems, you come back." Guy said, closing the door.

Ruben leaned toward the open window as he started the engine. "I will. I know where to find you." He tapped his hand a couple times on the steering wheel. "CJ, about what Mindy asked. She wanted you to find his mother."

"I know."

"I'm glad you guys decided to take root here. Stay put. If she's looking, you need to stay put."

"And if she's not?" CJ asked.

"Then I would believe the worst occurred. I can't imagine any parent not wanting to search for their child. Can you?" He put the car in gear, then with a simple wave and no more lingering goodbyes, Ruben backup and pulled away.

"What now?" CJ asked.

"Right now, you are with Carter until they figure out what job to give you. You know they're trying to keep things normal when housekeeping is on the clock. Me, I'm reporting to the hardware store. I'm helping with the wall."

"Dad, do they really need it?"

"Honestly, son, maybe not now. But if the government doesn't get back on its feet, if law and order is determined by each area, then yep. They're gonna need it and maybe a whole lot more." Guy gave a swat to CJ's arm and walked off.

CJ stood alone, he could hear the squeaky wheel of the housekeeping cart.

Normalcy.

The town was trying its hardest to be normal in the wake of everything that had happened. Keep people busy.

CJ had really nothing on his plate for the day. Unlike his father, he wasn't handed a job. It was all new to him. Twenty-four hours earlier he wouldn't have imagined that he'd be stopping and finding a new home in a small New Mexico town. Because twenty-four hours earlier all he focused on was finding help for Mindy.

After that, CJ didn't really think about it. Now he had to. With his home gone, he had to find a safe place with Carter. An area where the child stood a chance amidst all the chaos and destruction in the world. A situation that climatically would get worse.

Dig in, brace for it, and hope for that best while keeping his son safe and alive.

That was all CJ could do, beyond that … he just didn't know.

It was a whole new world. CJ was content keeping Carter from it and with his father behind the helm of walling them in, Lordsburg was a good place to be.

EPILOGUE

FOUR MONTHS LATER

Sergeant Joe Lawson drove Charles to Midland and had stayed by his side ever since. Helping out as best as he could. So when Charles asked him to drive him back to Cheyenne Mountain, he didn't hesitate to do so.

Midland, despite how big the refugees' displacement camp was, ended up being over crowded. There was nothing they could do about it. It wouldn't be long, both he and Charles knew, before the camps became a breeding ground for crimes.

They were already on their way.

Food resources were scarce. Fighting was a daily event, and disease spread quickly.

Medically they couldn't keep up. For a while, in the beginning help was promised from the countries across the globe that weren't touched. That help never arrived.

It didn't take long for the cities that were still standing, the areas still functioning to fraction off on their own.

Unwritten laws were in effect. People didn't travel between communities unless they had good cause and they better have bartering power to get in.

Midland didn't operate like that, at least for the time being, it was a free state.

How fast, how incredibly fast it all fell apart.

"We'll bring some of them back," Charles said.

"Oh, I know."

"We'll try to get the others help."

"I know that too. I'm really curious. I had friends there."

"So did I."

Communications with Cheyenne were never restored, they never heard from them again. The weather was already dangerously cold and winter had taken hold by the end of September. It wouldn't be long before the light snow that fell turned into crippling blizzards. The few scientists that remained and spoke up were predicting that.

Unfortunately, by the time they reached Colorado, the bad weather had already begun and they never were able to get close to Cheyenne. Without road crews or cars driving, the streets were impassible, most of the roads weren't even roads any longer.

When they stopped the truck to turn around, Lawson cleared a section of the snow, he wanted to see if they veered of the highway somehow because it felt rough. When he did, he uncovered what looked like coal. The surface below the snow was rigid and black.

"What is it?" Charles asked.

"The ash turned to stone," Lawson replied. "Remember they said if it mixed with rain. I guess it did."

Charles shuffled his foot in the snow. "It's everywhere."

"This whole area."

"Buried."

Lawson lifted his head. "We need to go, it's coming down pretty good and I don't want our tracks to get buried."

Charles nodded and got back in the truck. Even with a Humvee they didn't want to chance it.

They gave an effort, making it within hours of Cheyenne. Perhaps in the future they would try again, but until then, unless communications were restored, they probably never would know what happened to the former president and the five hundred and four people that remained at Cheyenne Mountain.

One of the things that Ruben did, like many others searching for family, was they made return trips to different camps and small towns. The numbers changed daily. People passed through, and even though everything seemed divided, one thing remained. Everyone kept track of who passed through their town.

He never did find his son Stew at Texas A&M. His dorm building was destroyed and Ruben spent a week going through that rubble. He found Stew's baseball cap, at least he believed it was Stew's. He never was without that Las Vegas cap. It had blood on it, but that meant nothing to Ruben. He wasn't giving up until he knew one way or another.

What else did he have to do?

He went from town to town, camp to camp. The truck had held up well, and he gathered a lot of items to barter with by giving people rides.

He thought about taking a break, going back to Lordsburg. Settle a bit, get his body back in shape. It had taken a beating on the road. The weather was getting bad and soon he wouldn't be able to search. Until he reached that point he'd keep going. He had been back there when he passed through to go to Tucson once. Guy gave him a hard time, jokingly, then let him pass. Only after he stayed the night and rested.

He was on his fourth time through his places to check, and was glad Midland was next. It was one of the only places remaining that didn't ask for anything to check the registry.

However, when he arrived, that didn't stop Ruben from grabbing a pair of gloves to trade. The lines were always long, and sometimes just something small would bump him up a space or two. Like others, he had the searching thing down to a science. It still didn't stop the surprises from popping up every now and again.

Kylie bounced back and forth, blew into her hands to try to warm them through the tattered gloves. Four hours in that line, and it wasn't that long. She just wished there was a room somewhere with the registry logs so people could search for themselves.

But they were almost there, they were next in line.

Every city, town or place they went was a challenger. Kylie and Tom were what people called Road Warriors. They walked most of the time and bartered rides the rest.

They dragged around their belongings in the vertical shopping carts, slept wherever they could make camp

"Mexico," Tom said. "I really think we need to try Mexico."

"Oh, I don't know."

"Kylie, we've been doing this for months. You heard what they said, a lot of people went to Mexico. We should try Mexico."

"What do we have to barter?"

"We have that rum," Tom said. "And those cigarettes. Potatoes." He snapped his finger. "Bet they'll let us in with potatoes."

"Then how to we get out."

"We have lots of stuff. I say we hit Mexico." He watched Kylie blow on her hands. "It'll be warmer."

"Excuse me," a man walked up to her. "I see your gloves are bad. I'll give you a new pair for your place in line."

"No, thank you." Kylie replied.

"I'll take that deal." Someone else in the next line said.

"Great." The man walked to the next line.

"Like I'd give up my space." Kylie chuckled and finally stepped forward.

The woman in the line sighed out. "Last update was two weeks ago, if you were here after that, we have no new names."

"I wasn't," Kyle said.

"Last name?"

"Him and I are looking for different people, two different last names," Kylie said.

"That's fine, you first," the woman said.

"James. Last name James."

"Swell, that's a common name."

"The first names aren't," Kylie said. "There would two males with the name Carter. One an adult, one a boy and an older man …"

"Guy."

Kylie froze and looked slowly to her left. The glove man stared at her. "Excuse me?" she asked.

"Guy. Guy James. Is that the same one? World's oldest stoner?"

"Oh my God." Kylie gasped, nearly falling backwards. "You know them."

"I do. We traveled together. Carter, the dad goes by CJ."

"Good Lord," Tom said. "This is unreal."

The woman behind the desk looked up. "She doesn't need me now. Who are you looking for?"

Kylie stepped away from Tom and to the glove man. "Are they okay? Do you know?"

"Yeah, they're fine. All of them."

At first her hand shot to her mouth emotionally then Kylie shrieked and grabbed on to him, 'Thank you. Thank you. Do you know where they last were? Where I can head?"

"They're still there. In fact … maybe it is time I went back there. Let me check the registry for my boy and I'll get you there."

Excitedly, Kylie nodded and spun to Tom who was talking to the woman. She felt bad that she received good news and Tom did not.

"No worries," he said to Kylie. "I'll find them. But you … your search may be over."

"Yes, maybe … I hope." She shifted her eyes to the glove man and had to calm herself, curb her enthusiasm. She'd not allow herself to happy or excited or any longer until she not only saw her son, but held him in her arms.

"Hinges would have worked better," the man said to Guy as they stood on the newly erected gate on the east side of town.

"Not better," Guy argued. "Easier. Our gates will not swing they will roll on tracks." Guy grunted with the final adjustment then brought the heavy gate forward, rolling it to a close.

There was a round of applause by the four men there.

Guy was proud of that gate the barricade spread across both lanes of the highway with the rolling gate on the approaching side.

The fifteen foot fence was constructed with a wooden frame, filled in with aluminum panels. Most of the materials were gathered from billboards and a local home superstore.

The roads were finished, at least the exits. A simple chain fence was erected on vulnerable areas around town. They would need more eventually, but Guy felt confident that with the weather increasingly getting bad, they wouldn't have many travelers.

Since the day he settled in Lordsburg, Guy stayed busy. Just like he was in the world before the events, he was a jack of all trades. Despite his self-proclaimed tremendous job on the fences, the crown he wore most proudly was that of a farmer.

At first he was just a worker bee, helping on the fences, by day and the green house at night. Then Guy pretty much took over. In a few months he went from the newbie in town, to one of the trusted.

Graham pulled up, just at that moment. He stepped from the car, then hands on hips, nodded proudly. "Looks great. The last one is done."

"It is," Guy said. "And we added a little extra." He walked to the door. "Peep hole." He opened a little square, "which also can serve as a gun hole."

"What about the crow's nest?" Graham asked.

"One thing at a time. Right now we are perching the lookouts up on the ladder."

"All day and night."

"We take turns. I definitely want to add the peep hole and gun hole to the west fence. In case them Cotton City boys come back up here. Shoot them before they open their mouths."

"Guy, come one, that wasn't their fault."

"You don't think?" Guy asked. "They tried to trade off that sick pig. In fact they *did* trade that sick pig. I told you, didn't I? I said, 'that pig is sick'."

"You did." Graham nodded.

"But nope. You didn't listen. You gave them ten gallons of diesel and a bunch of other stuff, including an ounce of my freshly dried finest. And what did we get?"

"A sick pig."

"No, thirty-three cases of the swine flu," Guy corrected. "Thirty three. That's once percent. That's epidemic. They started an epidemic."

"It was an accident."

"It was deliberate. The new world version of a biological weapon. Good thing Doc Mike was on the ball."

"Good thing. You done griping?" Graham asked.

"Yes."

"You know, because I hear this all the time."

"I'm old. I repeat myself."

"You're not that old," Graham said. "Anyhow. You were right. Smaller batch the better. We're priming the brew now. Should gave five gallons worth of bottles in couple hours."

"Hot damn. That's great news. We'll crack a few open tonight. Just don't tell CJ. He wastes beer, is a lightweight and a terrible drunk."

Graham laughed. "Sounds good. And more good news.... That still you made ... Reggie thinks he'll have the moonshine ready in a week."

"Getting better. You know damn well, one bottle of moonshine and a six pack is gonna yield us that basket of onions and peppers from Vinwar, we need them before winter sets in."

"I want … I want to send a salvaging crew out one more time. At least once before the weather gets bad. We never snow in these parts, so this will be interesting."

"Agreed. Should put CJ on a crew or me. We both know how to drive in the snow."

"Will do. I'll start …"

"Guy!" one of his men called out from the latter.

Guy turned around. "What's up?"

"Vehicle."

Guy walked to the fence and opened the peep hole, looking out. He recognized the beat up pick-up truck. "Oh, wow, that's Ruben. Ruben's back."

"Think he's back for the winter?" Graham asked.

"I do." Guy slid open the fence slightly. "Be good to have him here." He stepped out from the fence and waved as the truck pulled closer.

"Is there someone with him?" Graham asked.

"Yeah," Guy said softly. "Be vigilant in case he's been forced to get us to open."

Ruben stopped the truck ten feet from Guy.

It was an odd move and Guy peered closely at the truck and passenger seat. He squinted, trying to get a clear view, then after Ruben stepped out with a smile and a wave, the passenger door opened.

Guy couldn't move. He froze when he saw Kylie step out. "Holy Mother of God.

CJ just wanted to get home. That was all. It was cold, his fingers were numb. He had just gotten back from a difficult trade in Bowie for rice and nearly froze to death because the heater in the van didn't work.

He hated trading, he really did. But it seemed there was rarely any single job for CJ to do. They shuffled him around weekly. When he was asked what he did for a living, and he mentioned, 'painter', he was surprised that the reaction wasn't better. It was an honest job, but no one got it. They said they'd keep him busy with other stuff, but if he wanted, he could run an art class once a week as a morale booster.

Sometimes he worked at the hotel, but there were never any guests. He worked at the diner, at ration center. He wanted to work on the fences, but Guy wouldn't let him. Nor would his father let him near the greenhouse because he said CJ had a brown thumb.

He didn't mind making road trips to areas abandoned. Towns that were affected by the quakes or meteor. CJ had a niche for finding things, often swearing he was channeling Mindy. They were able to salvage some really good stuff. Even going forty miles north they found warehouses people seemed to forget about.

They had to stockpile, for both trade and survival. Winter was at hand, and it looked like any attempts at crops would be futile for a long time.

On this day it was a simple trade that was miserable. The old guy with the rice was just moving so slow, and was wishy-washy about the trade. After dropping off the van at the depot, he picked up Carter from a friend's house and headed through town to the two bedroom trailer he shared with his father near the far end of Lordsburg.

He just wanted to get there. But Abby followed them and was relentless.

"It's not important, Abby," CJ said. "Can I just go home?"

"Can you just think about it?" she asked.

"Why are you even doing this?" CJ stopped walking.

"Dad." Carter tugged his hand.

"In a second," CJ replied.

"Counsel wants it. They think it will boost morale. Not … not that your art class isn't wonderful."

CJ grumbled. "I'm cold. I just want to get my son home."

"Dad."

"Can you at least think about it? I so need a lead for Sound of Music."

"Oh my God. Ask me when I'm warm." CJ felt the tug to his hand. "What Carter?"

"Is that mom?"

Shocked.

CJ spun to where Carter pointed.

Had she not been walking with his father, CJ wouldn't have recognized her.

The red knit cap was bulky and large burying most of her face, and she wore a green plaid coat, tied at the waist with a rope. CJ released Carter's hand and the boy ran top speed to her, calling out, "Mom!" over and over.

Kylie raced his way as well, but only a short distance. She fell to her knees and Carter ran into her nearly knocking her over.

Kylie held him rocking him for a few seconds, then placed her hands on Carter's face, looking at him, feeling him and kissing him.

"My boy, my boy, my baby boy," she cried, "My baby boy. Mommy missed you. Mommy missed you so much."

CJ moved closer at a slow pace. He noticed Ruben was with his father, and another man as CJ stood behind Carter not wanting to interrupt the reunion. He knew how he felt after two days of not seeing Carter, he could only imagine how Kylie felt.

She sniffled and looked up to CJ, then stood. "Thank you for taking care of him."

"Oh my God, Kylie." CJ grabbed hold of her and brought him into his arms. Even though it had been years since the divorce, years since he held her, she was bone thin. "You're alive."

She sniffed and stepped back. "Ruben told me everything. All that you guys went through." She looked CJ then to Guy. "And you kept our son alive. He looks so healthy."

"We have it pretty good here," CJ said. "Now you will too."

Her lips pouted as she held back tears. "I'm so glad you stayed put. I never would have found you. Especially without Ruben."

"Right place at the right time," Ruben said.

"This is my friend, Tom," Kylie pulled him forward. "He rescued me in the beginning and has been with me ever since. He's searching for his family."

Tom shook CJ's hand. "I'm so happy for Kylie. You know, we went around this place twice. Once headed west, the other headed east. We never approached the gates because we heard not to come near. I wish we had."

"Better late than never," CJ said.

Abby cleared her throat and stepped forward, "My name is Abby. CJ, why don't I take them to get them some warm clothes and some food. I'll take them to my house. It's more comfortable."

Guy crinkled his brow. "What do you mean more comfortable? You got the same trailer as we do."

Abby whispered. "Mine is cleaner."

With an 'eh' Guy tossed out his hand in a wave.

"CJ is that okay?" Abby asked.

"Yes. Yes, thank you," CJ said. "I'll be right there."

Abby placed her arm around Kylie as support, as Kylie took Carter's hand. She looked over her shoulder once to CJ as they walked down the street.

CJ released the breath he held and faced Ruben. "This is unreal. How?"

"Timing." Ruben shrugged.

"Are you just dropping them off?" Guy asked. "Or are you staying?"

"I'm going to stay a little while. There's talk that it snowed pretty bad up north. Roads will be rough in the snow," Ruben said. "I was talking to Tom. He's still searching for his family. I think him and I will work together on looking."

"No luck finding Stew?" Guy asked.

"Not yet. And I emphasized the word yet. I mean, miracles can happen, right?" Ruben said. "Look what happened today."

"Absolutely. And you're just in time for another miracle." Guy slapped his hand on Ruben's back. "We have beer."

"No way."

"Yep. Next week … moonshine."

"How about your pot?"

"Finest in the nation," Guy boasted. Hand still on Ruben's back, he began to lead him, following Abby and Kylie. He paused. "CJ, you coming?"

"Yes, in a second. Go on."

Five minutes earlier, CJ couldn't wait to get to his home. Now he needed a moment to stop and take it all in. It was a complete and utter shock to his physical and emotional being when he saw Kylie. It wasn't real at first, because he never in a million years believed it would happen.

Yet there she was. It was the happiest he had seen his son in a very long time. That made CJ happy.

He hated what happened to the world, even resented the life he had to live. For months he felt frustrated, restless, now suddenly he felt sense of resolve. There was a sense of completion. Even though Kylie hadn't been his wife in a long time, she as the mother of his son and family nonetheless.

After seeing her and how worn she looked, he knew how good they had it in Lordsburg.

He was hit with a truth he had been denying.

They were all lucky.

Billions had died … they did. And they didn't just survive, they were living.

The country had become a vast wasteland, a good portion of which, CJ had seen. More than likely things would deteriorate more, they'd plan on that. For the time being, within the fenced in walls of a protected tiny blip on a map, there was an abundance of life.

It was time CJ started to appreciate that.

From that moment on, he promised himself he would.

Standing there in the middle of the street, traces of snow falling, he thought of Mindy, all that she said about Kylie and how insistent she was. CJ looked up to the sky. "You were right," he said. "You were right."

He had been standing there so long, his father and Ruben were fading from sight. With a quick pace, he moved to reach them, and did so with a smile on his face.

Once together at Abby's, CJ planned to spend time with family and be grateful for the reunion that was nothing short of a miracle. Then maybe, just maybe, because he knew it would irk his father, he'd even have one of those beers.

Thank you so much for reading this book. I hope you found it fun and enjoyed it.

Please visit my website www.jacquelinedruga.com and sign up for my mailing list for updates, freebies, new releases and giveaways. And, don't forget my new Kindle club!

Your support is invaluable to me. I welcome and respond to your feedback. Please feel free to email me at Jacqueline@jacquelinedruga.com

www.ingramcontent.com/pod-product-compliance
Lightning Source LLC
Chambersburg PA
CBHW051254250726
48656CB00004B/1286